Robert Louis Stevenson

Songs of Travel and other Verses

Robert Louis Stevenson

Songs of Travel and other Verses

ISBN/EAN: 9783743314153

Manufactured in Europe, USA, Canada, Australia, Japa

Cover: Foto ©Thomas Meinert / pixelio.de

Manufactured and distributed by brebook publishing software
(www.brebook.com)

Robert Louis Stevenson

Songs of Travel and other Verses

SONGS OF TRAVEL

AND OTHER VERSES

WORKS BY ROBERT LOUIS STEVENSON

AN INLAND VOYAGE
EDINBURGH: PICTURESQUE NOTES
TRAVELS WITH A DONKEY
VIRGINIBUS PUERISQUE
FAMILIAR STUDIES OF MEN AND BOOKS
NEW ARABIAN NIGHTS
TREASURE ISLAND
THE SILVERADO SQUATTERS
A CHILD'S GARDEN OF VERSES
STRANGE CASE OF DR. JEKYLL AND MR. HYDE
PRINCE OTTO
THE MERRY MEN
KIDNAPPED
UNDERWOODS
MEMORIES AND PORTRAITS
THE BLACK ARROW
THE MASTER OF BALLANTRAE
BALLADS
FATHER DAMIEN: AN OPEN LETTER
ACROSS THE PLAINS
A FOOTNOTE TO HISTORY
ISLAND NIGHTS ENTERTAINMENTS
CATRIONA
WEIR OF HERMISTON
VAILIMA LETTERS
FABLES

(With Mrs. Stevenson)

THE DYNAMITER

(With Lloyd Osbourne)

THE WRONG BOX
THE WRECKER
THE EBB-TIDE

SONGS OF TRAVEL

AND OTHER VERSES

BY

ROBERT LOUIS STEVENSON

LONDON

CHATTO & WINDUS, PICCADILLY

1896

THE following collection of verses, written at various times and places, principally after the author's final departure from England in 1887, was sent home by him for publication some months before his death. He had tried them in several different orders and under several different titles, as "Songs and Notes of Travel," "Posthumous Poems," etc., and in the end left their naming and arrangement to the present editor, with the suggestion that they should be added as Book III. to future editions of "Underwoods." This suggestion it is proposed to carry out; but in the meantime, for the benefit of those who possess "Underwoods" in its original form, it has been thought desirable to publish them separately in the present volume. They have already been included in the Edinburgh Edition of the author's works.

S. C.

CONTENTS

vii

CONTENTS

I

THE VAGABOND

(To an air of Schubert)

Give to me the life I love,
   Let the lave go by me,
Give the jolly heaven above
   And the byway nigh me.
Bed in the bush with stars to see,
   Bread I dip in the river—
There's the life for a man like me,
   There's the life for ever.

Let the blow fall soon or late,
  Let what will be o'er me ;
Give the face of earth around
  And the road before me.
Wealth I seek not, hope nor love,
  Nor a friend to know me ;
All I seek, the heaven above
  And the road below me.

Or let autumn fall on me
  Where afield I linger,
Silencing the bird on tree,
  Biting the blue finger.
White as meal the frosty field—
  Warm the fireside haven—
Not to autumn will I yield,
  Not to winter even !

Let the blow fall soon or late,

Let what will be o'er me ;

Give the face of earth around,

And the road before me.

Wealth I ask not, hope nor love,

Nor a friend to know me ;

All I ask, the heaven above

And the road below me.

II

YOUTH AND LOVE—I

ONCE only by the garden gate
  Our lips we joined and parted.
I must fulfil an empty fate
  And travel the uncharted.

Hail and farewell! I must arise,
  Leave here the fatted cattle,
And paint on foreign lands and skies
  My Odyssey of battle.

The untented Kosmos my abode,
  I pass, a wilful stranger:

My mistress still the open road
    And the bright eyes of danger.

Come ill or well, the cross, the crown,
    The rainbow or the thunder,
I fling my soul and body down
    For God to plough them under.

III

To the heart of youth the world is a highwayside.
Passing for ever, he fares; and on either hand,
Deep in the gardens golden pavilions hide,
Nestle in orchard bloom, and far on the level land
Call him with lighted lamp in the eventide.

Thick as the stars at night when the moon is down,
Pleasures assail him. He to his nobler fate
Fares; and but waves a hand as he passes on,
Cries but a wayside word to her at the garden gate,
Sings but a boyish stave and his face is gone.

6

In dreams, unhappy, I behold you stand
      As heretofore :
The unremembered tokens in your hand
      Avail no more.

No more the morning glow, no more the grace,
      Enshrines, endears.
Cold beats the light of time upon your face
      And shows your tears.

He came and went.   Perchance you wept a while
      And then forgot.
Ah me ! but he that left you with a smile
      Forgets you not.

SHE rested by the Broken Brook
 She drank of Weary Well,
She moved beyond my lingering look,
 Ah, whither none can tell!

She came, she went. In other lands,
 Perchance in fairer skies,
Her hands shall cling with other hands,
 Her eyes to other eyes.

She vanished. In the sounding town,
 Will she remember too?
Will she recall the eyes of brown
 As I recall the blue?

THE infinite shining heavens
   Rose and I saw in the night
Uncountable angel stars
   Showering sorrow and light.

I saw them distant as heaven,
   Dumb and shining and dead,
And the idle stars of the night
   Were dearer to me than bread.

Night after night in my sorrow
   The stars stood over the sea,
Till lo! I looked in the dusk
   And a star had come down to me.

PLAIN as the glistering planets shine

    When winds have cleaned the skies,

Her love appeared, appealed for mine,

    And wantoned in her eyes.

Clear as the shining tapers burned

    On Cytherea's shrine,

Those brimming, lustrous beauties turned,

    And called and conquered mine.

The beacon-lamp that Hero lit

    No fairer shone on sea,

No plainlier summoned will and wit,

    Than hers encouraged me.

10

I thrilled to feel her influence near,
    I struck my flag at sight.
Her starry silence smote my ear
    Like sudden drums at night.

I ran as, at the cannon's roar,
    The troops the ramparts man—
As in the holy house of yore
    The willing Eli ran.

Here, lady, lo ! that servant stands
    You picked from passing men,
And should you need nor heart nor hands
    He bows and goes again.

To you, let snow and roses
  And golden locks belong.
These are the world's enslavers,
  Let these delight the throng.
For her of duskier lustre
  Whose favour still I wear,
The snow be in her kirtle,
  The rose be in her hair!

The hue of highland rivers
  Careering, full and cool,
From sable on to golden,
  From rapid on to pool—
The hue of heather-honey,
  The hue of honey-bees,
Shall tinge her golden shoulder,
  Shall gild her tawny knees.

12

LET Beauty awake in the morn from beautiful dreams,

    Beauty awake from rest !

    Let Beauty awake

    For Beauty's sake

In the hour when the birds awake in the brake

    And the stars are bright in the west !

Let Beauty awake in the eve from the slumber of day,

    Awake in the crimson eve !

    In the day's dusk end

    When the shades ascend,

Let her wake to the kiss of a tender friend

    To render again and receive !

X

I KNOW not how it is with you—
　　I love the first and last,
The whole field of the present view,
　　The whole flow of the past.

One tittle of the things that are,
　　Nor you should change nor I—
One pebble in our path—one star
　　In all our heaven of sky.

Our lives, and every day and hour,
　　One symphony appear :
One road, one garden—every flower
　　And every bramble dear.

I WILL make you brooches and toys for your delight

Of bird-song at morning and star-shine at night.

I will make a palace fit for you and me

Of green days in forests and blue days at sea.

I will make my kitchen, and you shall keep your room,

Where white flows the river and bright blows the broom,

And you shall wash your linen and keep your body white

In rainfall at morning and dewfall at night.

And this shall be for music when no one else is near,

The fine song for singing, the rare song to hear!

That only I remember, that only you admire,

Of the broad road that stretches and the roadside fire.

WE HAVE LOVED OF YORE

(To an air of Diabelli)

BERRIED brake and reedy island,

    Heaven below, and only heaven above,

Through the sky's inverted azure

    Softly swam the boat that bore our love.

           Bright were your eyes as the day ;

           Bright ran the stream,

           Bright hung the sky above.

Days of April, airs of Eden,

    How the glory died through golden hours,

And the shining moon arising,

    How the boat drew homeward filled with flowers !

Bright were your eyes in the night :

We have lived, my love—

O, we have loved, my love.

Frost has bound our flowing river,

    Snow has whitened all our island brake,

And beside the winter fagot

    Joan and Darby doze and dream and wake.

        Still, in the river of dreams

        Swims the boat of love—

        Hark ! chimes the falling oar !

And again in winter evens

    When on firelight dreaming fancy feeds,

In those ears of agèd lovers

    Love's own river warbles in the reeds.

        Love still the past, O my love !

        We have lived of yore,

        O, we have loved of yore.

XIII

MATER TRIUMPHANS

Son of my woman's body, you go, to the drum and fife,

To taste the colour of love and the other side of life—

From out of the dainty the rude, the strong from out of
the frail,

Eternally through the ages from the female comes the
male.

The ten fingers and toes, and the shell-like nail on each,

The eyes blind as gems and the tongue attempting speech ;

Impotent hands in my bosom, and yet they shall wield the
sword !

Drugged with slumber and milk, you wait the day of the
Lord.

18

Infant bridegroom, uncrowned king, unanointed priest,

Soldier, lover, explorer, I see you nuzzle the breast.

You that grope in my bosom shall load the ladies with
rings,

You, that came forth through the doors, shall burst the
doors of kings.

BRIGHT is the ring of words
 When the right man rings them,
Fair the fall of songs
 When the singer sings them.
Still they are carolled and said—
 On wings they are carried—
After the singer is dead
 And the maker buried.

Low as the singer lies
 In the field of heather,
Songs of his fashion bring
 The swains together.
And when the west is red
 With the sunset embers,
The lover lingers and sings
 And the maid remembers.

In the highlands, in the country places,

Where the old plain men have rosy faces,

And the young fair maidens

Quiet eyes;

Where essential silence cheers and blesses,

And for ever in the hill-recesses

Her more lovely music

Broods and dies.

O to mount again where erst I haunted;

Where the old red hills are bird-enchanted,

And the low green meadows

Bright with sward;

And when even dies, the million-tinted,

And the night has come, and planets glinted,

Lo, the valley hollow

Lamp-bestarred !

O to dream, O to awake and wander

There, and with delight to take and render,

Through the trance of silence,

Quiet breath ;

Lo ! for there, among the flowers and grasses,

Only the mightier movement sounds and passes ;

Only winds and rivers,

Life and death.

XVI

HOME no more home to me, whither must I wander?

    Hunger my driver, I go where I must.

Cold blows the winter wind over hill and heather;

    Thick drives the rain, and my roof is in the dust.

Loved of wise men was the shade of my roof-tree.

    The true word of welcome was spoken in the door—

Dear days of old, with the faces in the firelight,

    Kind folks of old, you come again no more.

Home was home then, my dear, full of kindly faces,

    Home was home then, my dear, happy for the child.

Fire and the windows bright glittered on the moorland;

    Song, tuneful song, built a palace in the wild.

Now, when day dawns on the brow of the moorland,
  Lone stands the house, and the chimney-stone is cold.
Lone let it stand, now the friends are all departed,
  The kind hearts, the true hearts, that loved the place of
    old.

Spring shall come, come again, calling up the moorfowl,
  Spring shall bring the sun and rain, bring the bees and
    flowers ;
Red shall the heather bloom over hill and valley,
  Soft flow the stream through the even-flowing hours ;
Fair the day shine as it shone on my childhood—
  Fair shine the day on the house with open door ;
Birds come and cry there and twitter in the chimney—
  But I go for ever and come again no more.

WINTER

In rigorous hours, when down the iron lane
The redbreast looks in vain
For hips and haws,
Lo, shining flowers upon my window-pane
The silver pencil of the winter draws.

When all the snowy hill
And the bare woods are still;
When snipes are silent in the frozen bogs,
And all the garden garth is whelmed in mire,
Lo, by the hearth, the laughter of the logs—
More fair than roses, lo, the flowers of fire!

Saranac Lake.

XVIII

THE stormy evening closes now in vain,

Loud wails the wind and beats the driving rain,

  While here in sheltered house

  With fire-ypainted walls,

  I hear the wind abroad,

  I hark the calling squalls—

'Blow, blow,' I cry, 'you burst your cheeks in vain!

Blow, blow,' I cry, 'my love is home again!'

Yon ship you chase perchance but yesternight

Bore still the precious freight of my delight,

  That here in sheltered house

  With fire-ypainted walls,

  Now hears the wind abroad,

  Now harks the calling squalls.

'Blow, blow,' I cry, 'in vain you rouse the sea,

My rescued sailor shares the fire with me!'

TO DR. HAKE

(On receiving a Copy of Verses)

In the belovèd hour that ushers day,

In the pure dew, under the breaking grey,

One bird, ere yet the woodland quires awake,

With brief réveillé summons all the brake :

Chirp, chirp, it goes ; nor waits an answer long ;

And that small signal fills the grove with song.

Thus on my pipe I breathed a strain or two ;

It scarce was music, but 'twas all I knew.

It was not music, for I lacked the art,

Yet what but frozen music filled my heart ?

27

Chirp, chirp, I went, nor hoped a nobler strain ;

But Heaven decreed I should not pipe in vain,

For, lo ! not far from there, in secret dale,

All silent, sat an ancient nightingale.

My sparrow notes he heard ; thereat awoke ;

And with a tide of song his silence broke.

TO ——

I KNEW thee strong and quiet like the hills ;
I knew thee apt to pity, brave to endure,
In peace or war a Roman full equipt ;
And just I knew thee, like the fabled kings
Who by the loud sea-shore gave judgment forth,
From dawn to eve, bearded and few of words.
What, what, was I to honour thee ?   A child ;
A youth in ardour but a child in strength,
Who after virtue's golden chariot-wheels
Runs ever panting, nor attains the goal.
So thought I, and was sorrowful at heart.

Since then my steps have visited that flood
Along whose shore the numerous footfalls cease,

The voices and the tears of life expire.

Thither the prints go down, the hero's way

Trod large upon the sand, the trembling maid's :

Nimrod that wound his trumpet in the wood,

And the poor, dreaming child, hunter of flowers,

That here his hunting closes with the great :

So one and all go down, nor aught returns.

For thee, for us, the sacred river waits,

For me, the unworthy, thee, the perfect friend ;

There Blame desists, there his unfaltering dogs

He from the chase recalls, and homeward rides ;

Yet Praise and Love pass over and go in.

So when, beside that margin, I discard

My more than mortal weakness, and with thee

Through that still land unfearing I advance :

If then at all we keep the touch of joy

Thou shalt rejoice to find me altered--I,

O Felix, to behold thee still unchanged.

THE morning drum-call on my eager ear
Thrills unforgotten yet; the morning dew
Lies yet undried along my field of noon.

But now I pause at whiles in what I do,
And count the bell, and tremble lest I hear
(My work untrimmed) the sunset gun too soon.

XXII

I HAVE trod the upward and the downward slope ;

I have endured and done in days before ;

I have longed for all, and bid farewell to hope ;

And I have lived and loved, and closed the door.

HE hears with gladdened heart the thunder
    Peal, and loves the falling dew ;
He knows the earth above and under—
    Sits and is content to view.

He sits beside the dying ember,
    God for hope and man for friend,
Content to see, glad to remember,
    Expectant of the certain end.

FAREWELL, fair day and fading light!

The clay-born here, with westward sight,

Marks the huge sun now downward soar.

Farewell.   We twain shall meet no more.

Farewell.   I watch with bursting sigh

My late contemned occasion die.

I linger useless in my tent:

Farewell, fair day, so foully spent!

Farewell, fair day.   If any God

At all consider this poor clod,

He who the fair occasion sent

Prepared and placed the impediment.

34

Let him diviner vengeance take—
Give me to sleep, give me to wake
Girded and shod, and bid me play
The hero in the coming day!

XXV

IF THIS WERE FAITH

God, if this were enough,

That I see things bare to the buff

And up to the buttocks in mire ;

That I ask nor hope nor hire,

Nut in the husk,

Nor dawn beyond the dusk,

Nor life beyond death :

God, if this were faith?

Having felt thy wind in my face

Spit sorrow and disgrace,

Having seen thine evil doom

In Golgotha and Khartoum,

And the brutes, the work of thine hands,

Fill with injustice lands

And stain with blood the sea :

If still in my veins the glee

Of the black night and the sun

And the lost battle, run :

If, an adept,

The iniquitous lists I still accept

With joy, and joy to endure and be withstood,

And still to battle and perish for a dream of good :

God, if that were enough ?

If to feel, in the ink of the slough,

And the sink of the mire,

Veins of glory and fire

Run through and transpierce and transpire,

And a secret purpose of glory in every part,

And the answering glory of battle fill my heart ;

To thrill with the joy of girded men

To go on for ever and fail and go on again,

And be mauled to the earth and arise,

And contend for the shade of a word and a thing not seen
    with the eyes :

With the half of a broken hope for a pillow at night

That somehow the right is the right

And the smooth shall bloom from the rough :

Lord, if that were enough ?

XXVI

MY WIFE

TRUSTY, dusky, vivid, true,

With eyes of gold and bramble-dew,

Steel-true and blade-straight,

The great artificer

Made my mate.

Honour, anger, valour, fire;

A love that life could never tire,

Death quench or evil stir,

The mighty master

Gave to her.

Teacher, tender, comrade, wife,

A fellow-farer true through life,

Heart-whole and soul-free

The august father

Gave to me.

XXVII

TO THE MUSE

RESIGN the rhapsody, the dream,
   To men of larger reach ;
Be ours the quest of a plain theme,
   The piety of speech.

As monkish scribes from morning break
   Toiled till the close of light,
Nor thought a day too long to make
   One line or letter bright :

We also with an ardent mind,
   Time, wealth, and fame forgot,

Our glory in our patience find
And skim, and skim the pot :

Till last, when round the house we hear
The evensong of birds,
One corner of blue heaven appear
In our clear well of words.

Leave, leave it then, muse of my heart !
Sans finish and sans frame,
Leave unadorned by needless art
The picture as it came.

TO AN ISLAND PRINCESS

SINCE long ago, a child at home,

I read and longed to rise and roam,

Where'er I went, whate'er I willed,

One promised land my fancy filled.

Hence the long roads my home I made ;

Tossed much in ships ; have often laid

Below the uncurtained sky my head,

Rain-deluged and wind-buffeted :

And many a thousand hills I crossed

And corners turned—Love's labour lost,

Till, Lady, to your isle of sun

I came, not hoping; and, like one

Snatched out of blindness, rubbed my eyes,

And hailed my promised land with cries.

Yes, Lady, here I was at last;

Here found I all I had forecast:

The long roll of the sapphire sea

That keeps the land's virginity;

The stalwart giants of the wood

Laden with toys and flowers and food;

The precious forest pouring out

To compass the whole town about;

The town itself with streets of lawn,

Loved of the moon, blessed by the dawn,

Where the brown children all the day

Keep up a ceaseless noise of play,

Play in the sun, play in the rain,

Nor ever quarrel or complain ;—

And late at night, in the woods of fruit,

Hark! do you hear the passing flute?

I threw one look to either hand,

And knew I was in Fairyland.

And yet one point of being so

I lacked.   For, Lady (as you know),

Whoever by his might of hand,

Won entrance into Fairyland,

Found always with admiring eyes

A Fairy princess kind and wise.

It was not long I waited ; soon

Upon my threshold, in broad noon,

Gracious and helpful, wise and good,

The Fairy Princess Moë stood.[1]

Tantira, Tahiti, Nov. 5, 1888.

---

[1] This is the same Princess Moë whose charms of person and disposition have been recorded by the late Lord Pembroke in *South Sea Bubbles*, and by M. Pierre Loti in the *Mariage de Loti*.

XXIX

TO KALAKAUA

(With a present of a Pearl)

THE Silver Ship, my King—that was her name

In the bright islands whence your fathers came[1]—

The Silver Ship, at rest from winds and tides,

Below your palace in your harbour rides:

And the seafarers, sitting safe on shore,

Like eager merchants count their treasures o'er.

One gift they find, one strange and lovely thing,

Now doubly precious since it pleased a king.

The right, my liege, is ancient as the lyre

For bards to give to kings what kings admire.

---

[1] The yacht *Casco* had been so called by the people of Fakarava in the Paumotus.

'Tis mine to offer for Apollo's sake ;

And since the gift is fitting, yours to take.

To golden hands the golden pearl I bring :

The ocean jewel to the island king.

Honolulu, Feb. 3, 1889.

XXX

TO PRINCESS KAIULANI

[Written in April to Kaiulani in the April of her age; and at Waikiki, within easy walk of Kaiulani's banyan! When she comes to my land and her father's, and the rain beats upon the window (as I fear it will), let her look at this page; it will be like a weed gathered and pressed at home; and she will remember her own islands, and the shadow of the mighty tree; and she will hear the peacocks screaming in the dusk and the wind blowing in the palms; and she will think of her father sitting there alone.—R. L. S.]

FORTH from her land to mine she goes,

The island maid, the island rose,

Light of heart and bright of face:

The daughter of a double race.

Her islands here, in Southern sun,

Shall mourn their Kaiulani gone,

And I, in her dear banyan shade,

Look vainly for my little maid.

But our Scots islands far away

Shall glitter with unwonted day,

And cast for once their tempests by

To smile in Kaiulani's eye.

Honolulu.

TO MOTHER MARYANNE

To see the infinite pity of this place,

The mangled limb, the devastated face,

The innocent sufferer smiling at the rod—

A fool were tempted to deny his God.

He sees, he shrinks.   But if he gaze again,

Lo, beauty springing from the breast of pain !

He marks the sisters on the mournful shores ;

And even a fool is silent and adores.

Guest House, Kalawao, Molokai.

XXXII

IN MEMORIAM E. H.

I KNEW a silver head was bright beyond compare,
I knew a queen of toil with a crown of silver hair.
Garland of valour and sorrow, of beauty and renown,
Life, that honours the brave, crowned her himself with the
   crown.

The beauties of youth are frail, but this was a jewel of age.
Life, that delights in the brave, gave it himself for a gage.
Fair was the crown to behold, and beauty its poorest part—
At once the scar of the wound and the order pinned on the
   heart.

The beauties of man are frail, and the silver lies in the dust,
And the queen that we call to mind sleeps with the brave
   and the just;
Sleeps with the weary at length ; but, honoured and ever fair,
Shines in the eye of the mind the crown of the silver hair.

   Honolulu.

XXXIII

TO MY WIFE

(*A Fragment*)

Long must elapse ere you behold again

Green forest frame the entry of the lane—

The wild lane with the bramble and the brier,

The year-old cart-tracks perfect in the mire,

The wayside smoke, perchance, the dwarfish huts,

And ramblers' donkey drinking from the ruts :—

Long ere you trace how deviously it leads,

Back from man's chimneys and the bleating meads

To the woodland shadow, to the sylvan hush,

When but the brooklet chuckles in the brush—

Back from the sun and bustle of the vale

To where the great voice of the nightingale

Fills all the forest like a single room,

And all the banks smell of the golden broom ;

So wander on until the eve descends.

And back returning to your firelit friends,

You see the rosy sun, despoiled of light,

Hung, caught in thickets, like a schoolboy's kite.

Here from the sea the unfruitful sun shall rise,

Bathe the bare deck and blind the unshielded eyes ;

The allotted hours aloft shall wheel in vain

And in the unpregnant ocean plunge again.

Assault of squalls that mock the watchful guard,

And pluck the bursting canvas from the yard,

And senseless clamour of the calm, at night

Must mar your slumbers.   By the plunging light,

In beetle-haunted, most unwomanly bower

Of the wild-swerving cabin, hour by hour . . .

Schooner ' Equator.'

XXXIV

TO MY OLD FAMILIARS

Do you remember—can we e'er forget?—

How, in the coiled perplexities of youth,

In our wild climate, in our scowling town,

We gloomed and shivered, sorrowed, sobbed and feared?

The belching winter wind, the missile rain,

The rare and welcome silence of the snows,

The laggard morn, the haggard day, the night,

The grimy spell of the nocturnal town,

Do you remember?—Ah, could one forget!

As when the fevered sick that all night long

Listed the wind intone, and hear at last

The ever-welcome voice of chanticleer
Sing in the bitter hour before the dawn,—
With sudden ardour, these desire the day:
So sang in the gloom of youth the bird of hope;
So we, exulting, hearkened and desired.
For lo! as in the palace porch of life
We huddled with chimeras, from within—
How sweet to hear!—the music swelled and fell,
And through the breach of the revolving doors
What dreams of splendour blinded us and fled!

I have since then contended and rejoiced;
Amid the glories of the house of life
Profoundly entered, and the shrine beheld:
Yet when the lamp from my expiring eyes
Shall dwindle and recede, the voice of love
Fall insignificant on my closing ears,
What sound shall come but the old cry of the wind
In our inclement city? what return

But the image of the emptiness of youth,

Filled with the sound of footsteps and that voice

Of discontent and rapture and despair?

So, as in darkness, from the magic lamp,

The momentary pictures gleam and fade

And perish, and the night resurges—these

Shall I remember, and then all forget.

Apemama.

XXXV

THE tropics vanish, and meseems that I,

From Halkerside, from topmost Allermuir,

Or steep Caerketton, dreaming gaze again.

Far set in fields and woods, the town I see

Spring gallant from the shallows of her smoke,

Cragged, spired, and turreted, her virgin fort

Beflagged. About, on seaward-drooping hills,

New folds of city glitter. Last, the Forth

Wheels ample waters set with sacred isles,

And populous Fife smokes with a score of towns.

There, on the sunny frontage of a hill,

Hard by the house of kings, repose the dead,

My dead, the ready and the strong of word.

56

Their works, the salt-encrusted, still survive ;

The sea bombards their founded towers ; the night

Thrills pierced with their strong lamps.   The artificers,

One after one, here in this grated cell,

Where the rain erases, and the rust consumes,

Fell upon lasting silence.   Continents

And continental oceans intervene ;

A sea uncharted, on a lampless isle,

Environs and confines their wandering child

In vain.   The voice of generations dead

Summons me, sitting distant, to arise,

My numerous footsteps nimbly to retrace,

And, all mutation over, stretch me down

In that denoted city of the dead.

Apemama.

XXXVI

TO S. C.

I HEARD the pulse of the besieging sea
Throb far away all night.   I heard the wind
Fly crying and convulse tumultuous palms.
I rose and strolled.   The isle was all bright sand,
And flailing fans and shadows of the palm ;
The heaven all moon and wind and the blind vault ;
The keenest planet slain, for Venus slept.

The king, my neighbour, with his host of wives,
Slept in the precinct of the palisade ;
Where single, in the wind, under the moon,
Among the slumbering cabins, blazed a fire,
Sole street-lamp and the only sentinel.

58

To other lands and nights my fancy turned--

To London first, and chiefly to your house,

The many-pillared and the well-beloved.

There yearning fancy lighted ; there again

In the upper room I lay, and heard far off

The unsleeping city murmur like a shell ;

The muffled tramp of the Museum guard

Once more went by me ; I beheld again

Lamps vainly brighten the dispeopled street ;

Again I longed for the returning morn,

The awaking traffic, the bestirring birds,

The consentaneous trill of tiny song

That weaves round monumental cornices

A passing charm of beauty.   Most of all,

For your light foot I wearied, and your knock

That was the glad réveillé of my day.

Lo, now, when to your task in the great house

At morning through the portico you pass,

One moment glance, where by the pillared wall

Far-voyaging island gods, begrimed with smoke,

Sit now unworshipped, the rude monument

Of faiths forgot and races undivined :

Sit now disconsolate, remembering well

The priest, the victim, and the songful crowd,

The blaze of the blue noon, and that huge voice,

Incessant, of the breakers on the shore.

As far as these from their ancestral shrine,

So far, so foreign, your divided friends

Wander, estranged in body, not in mind.

Apemama.

XXXVII

THE HOUSE OF TEMBINOKA

[At my departure from the island of Apemama, for which you will look in vain in most atlases, the King and I agreed, since we both set up to be in the poetical way, that we should celebrate our separation in verse. Whether or not his Majesty has been true to his bargain, the laggard posts of the Pacific may perhaps inform me in six months, perhaps not before a year. The following lines represent my part of the contract, and it is hoped, by their pictures of strange manners, they may entertain a civilised audience. Nothing throughout has been invented or exaggerated ; the lady herein referred to as the author's muse has confined herself to stringing into rhyme facts or legends that I saw or heard during two months' residence upon the island.—R. L. S.]

ENVOI

Let us, who part like brothers, part like bards ;

And you in your tongue and measure, I in mine,

Our now division duly solemnise.

61

Unlike the strains, and yet the theme is one :

The strains unlike, and how unlike their fate !

You to the blinding palace-yard shall call

The prefect of the singers, and to him,

Listening devout, your valedictory verse

Deliver ; he, his attribute fulfilled,

To the island chorus hand your measures on,

Wed now with harmony: so them, at last,

Night after night, in the open hall of dance,

Shall thirty matted men, to the clapped hand,

Intone and bray and bark.   Unfortunate !

Paper and print alone shall honour mine.

THE SONG

LET now the King his ear arouse

And toss the bosky ringlets from his brows,

The while, our bond to implement,

My muse relates and praises his descent.

I

Bride of the shark, her valour first I sing
Who on the lone seas quickened of a King.
She, from the shore and puny homes of men,
Beyond the climber's sea-discerning ken,
Swam, led by omens; and devoid of fear,
Beheld her monstrous paramour draw near.
She gazed; all round her to the heavenly pale,
The simple sea was void of isle or sail—
Sole overhead the unsparing sun was reared—
When the deep bubbled and the brute appeared.
But she, secure in the decrees of fate,
Made strong her bosom and received the mate,
And, men declare, from that marine embrace
Conceived the virtues of a stronger race.

II

Her stern descendant next I praise,
Survivor of a thousand frays :—

63

In the hall of tongues who ruled the throng;

Led and was trusted by the strong;

And when spears were in the wood,

Like a tower of vantage stood :—

Whom, not till seventy years had sped,

Unscarred of breast, erect of head,

Still light of step, still bright of look,

The hunter, Death, had overtook.

III

His sons, the brothers twain, I sing,

Of whom the elder reigned a King.

No Childeric he, yet much declined

From his rude sire's imperious mind,

Until his day came when he died,

He lived, he reigned, he versified.

But chiefly him I celebrate

That was the pillar of the state,

Ruled, wise of word and bold of mien,

The peaceful and the warlike scene;

And played alike the leader's part

In lawful and unlawful art.

His soldiers with emboldened ears

Heard him laugh among the spears.

He could deduce from age to age

The web of island parentage;

Best lay the rhyme, best lead the dance,

For any festal circumstance:

And fitly fashion oar and boat,

A palace or an armour coat.

None more availed than he to raise

The strong, suffumigating blaze,

Or knot the wizard leaf: none more,

Upon the untrodden windward shore

Of the isle, beside the beating main,

To cure the sickly and constrain,

With muttered words and waving rods,

The gibbering and the whistling gods.

But he, though thus with hand and head
He ruled, commanded, charmed, and led,
And thus in virtue and in might
Towered to contemporary sight—
Still in fraternal faith and love,
Remained below to reach above,
Gave and obeyed the apt command,
Pilot and vassal of the land.

IV

My Tembinok' from men like these
Inherited his palaces,
His right to rule, his powers of mind,
His cocoa-islands sea-enshrined.
Stern bearer of the sword and whip,
A master passed in mastership,
He learned, without the spur of need,
To write, to cipher, and to read ;
From all that touch on his prone shore

66

Augments his treasury of lore,

Eager in age as erst in youth

To catch an art, to learn a truth,

To paint on the internal page

A clearer picture of the age.

His age, you say ?   But ah, not so !

In his lone isle of long ago,

A royal Lady of Shalott,

Sea-sundered, he beholds it not ;

He only hears it far away.

The stress of equatorial day

He suffers ; he records the while

The vapid annals of the isle ;

Slaves bring him praise of his renown,

Or cackle of the palm-tree town ;

The rarer ship and the rare boat

He marks ; and only hears remote,

Where thrones and fortunes rise and reel,

The thunder of the turning wheel.

V

For the unexpected tears he shed

At my departing, may his lion head

Not whiten, his revolving years

No fresh occasion minister of tears ;

At book or cards, at work or sport,

Him may the breeze across the palace court

For ever fan ; and swelling near

For ever the loud song divert his ear.

Schooner 'Equator,' at Sea.

XXXVIII

THE WOODMAN

In all the grove, nor stream nor bird
Nor aught beside my blows was heard,
And the woods wore their noonday dress—
The glory of their silentness.
From the island summit to the seas,
Trees mounted, and trees drooped, and trees
Groped upward in the gaps.   The green
Inarboured talus and ravine
By fathoms.   By the multitude
The rugged columns of the wood
And bunches of the branches stood;
Thick as a mob, deep as a sea,
And silent as eternity.

With lowered axe, with backward head,

Late from this scene my labourer fled,

And with a ravelled tale to tell,

Returned.   Some denizen of hell,

Dead man or disinvested god,

Had close behind him peered and trod,

And triumphed when he turned to flee.

How different fell the lines with me !

Whose eye explored the dim arcade

Impatient of the uncoming shade—

Shy elf, or dryad pale and cold,

Or mystic lingerer from of old :

Vainly.   The fair and stately things,

Impassive as departed kings,

All still in the wood's stillness stood,

And dumb.   The rooted multitude

Nodded and brooded, bloomed and dreamed,

Unmeaning, undivined.   It seemed

No other art, no hope, they knew,

Than clutch the earth and seek the blue.

'Mid vegetable king and priest

And stripling, I (the only beast)

Was at the beast's work, killing; hewed

The stubborn roots across, bestrewed

The glebe with the dislustred leaves,

And bade the saplings fall in sheaves;

Bursting across the tangled math

A ruin that I called a path,

A Golgotha that, later on,

When rains had watered, and suns shone,

And seeds enriched the place, should bear

And be called garden.   Here and there,

I spied and plucked by the green hair

A foe more resolute to live,

The toothed and killing sensitive.

He, semi-conscious, fled the attack;

He shrank and tucked his branches back;

And straining by his anchor-strand,

Captured and scratched the rooting hand.

I saw him crouch, I felt him bite;

And straight my eyes were touched with sight.

I saw the wood for what it was:

The lost and the victorious cause,

The deadly battle pitched in line,

Saw silent weapons cross and shine:

Silent defeat, silent assault,

A battle and a burial vault.

Thick round me in the teeming mud

Brier and fern strove to the blood:

The hooked liana in his gin

Noosed his reluctant neighbours in:

There the green murderer throve and spread,

Upon his smothering victims fed,

And wantoned on his climbing coil.

Contending roots fought for the soil

Like frightened demons: with despair

Competing branches pushed for air.

Green conquerors from overhead

Bestrode the bodies of their dead :

The Caesars of the sylvan field,

Unused to fail, foredoomed to yield :

For in the groins of branches, lo !

The cancers of the orchid grow.

Silent as in the listed ring

Two chartered wrestlers strain and cling ;

Dumb as by yellow Hooghly's side

The suffocating captives died ;

So hushed the woodland warfare goes

Unceasing ; and the silent foes

Grapple and smother, strain and clasp

Without a cry, without a gasp.

Here also sound thy fans, O God,

Here too thy banners move abroad :

Forest and city, sea and shore,

And the whole earth, thy threshing-floor !

The drums of war, the drums of peace,
Roll through our cities without cease,
And all the iron halls of life
Ring with the unremitting strife.

The common lot we scarce perceive.
Crowds perish, we nor mark nor grieve:
The bugle calls—we mourn a few!
What corporal's guard at Waterloo?
What scanty hundreds more or less
In the man-devouring Wilderness?
What handful bled on Delhi ridge?
—See, rather, London, on thy bridge
The pale battalions trample by,
Resolved to slay, resigned to die.
Count, rather, all the maimed and dead
In the unbrotherly war of bread.
See, rather, under sultrier skies
What vegetable Londons rise,

And teem, and suffer without sound :

Or in your tranquil garden ground,

Contented, in the falling gloom,

Saunter and see the roses bloom.

That these might live, what thousands died !

All day the cruel hoe was plied ;

The ambulance barrow rolled all day ;

Your wife, the tender, kind, and gay,

Donned her long gauntlets, caught the spud,

And bathed in vegetable blood ;

And the long massacre now at end,

See ! where the lazy coils ascend,

See, where the bonfire sputters red

At even, for the innocent dead.

Why prate of peace ? when, warriors all,

We clank in harness into hall,

And ever bare upon the board

Lies the necessary sword.

In the green field or quiet street,

Besieged we sleep, beleaguered eat;

Labour by day and wake o' nights,

In war with rival appetites.

The rose on roses feeds; the lark

On larks.   The sedentary clerk

All morning with a diligent pen

Murders the babes of other men;

And like the beasts of wood and park,

Protects his whelps, defends his den.

Unshamed the narrow aim I hold;

I feed my sheep, patrol my fold;

Breathe war on wolves and rival flocks,

A pious outlaw on the rocks

Of God and morning; and when time

Shall bow, or rivals break me, climb

Where no undubbed civilian dares,

In my war harness, the loud stairs

Of honour ; and my conqueror

Hail me a warrior fallen in war.

Vailima.

TROPIC RAIN

As the single pang of the blow, when the metal is mingled
 well,

Rings and lives and resounds in all the bounds of the bell,

So the thunder above spoke with a single tongue,

So in the heart of the mountain the sound of it rumbled
 and clung.

Sudden the thunder was drowned—quenched was the levin
 light—

And the angel-spirit of rain laughed out loud in the night.

Loud as the maddened river raves in the cloven glen,

Angel of rain ! you laughed and leaped on the roofs of men;

And the sleepers sprang in their beds, and joyed and feared
    as you fell.

You struck, and my cabin quailed; the roof of it roared
    like a bell,

You spoke, and at once the mountain shouted and shook
    with brooks.

You ceased, and the day returned, rosy, with virgin looks.

And methought that beauty and terror are only one, not
    two;

And the world has room for love, and death, and thunder,
    and dew;

And all the sinews of hell slumber in summer air;

And the face of God is a rock, but the face of the rock is
    fair.

Beneficent streams of tears flow at the finger of pain;

And out of the cloud that smites, beneficent rivers of rain.

   Vailima.

AN END OF TRAVEL

Let now your soul in this substantial world
Some anchor strike.   Be here the body moored ;—
This spectacle immutably from now
The picture in your eye ; and when time strikes,
And the green scene goes on the instant blind—
The ultimate helpers, where your horse to-day
Conveyed you dreaming, bear your body dead.

Vailima.

XLI

WE uncommiserate pass into the night

From the loud banquet, and departing leave

A tremor in men's memories, faint and sweet

And frail as music.   Features of our face,

The tones of the voice, the touch of the loved hand,

Perish and vanish, one by one, from earth :

Meanwhile, in the hall of song, the multitude

Applauds the new performer.   One, perchance,

One ultimate survivor lingers on,

And smiles, and to his ancient heart recalls

The long forgotten.   Ere the morrow die,

He too, returning, through the curtain comes,

And the new age forgets us and goes on.

SING me a song of a lad that is gone,
    Say, could that lad be I?
Merry of soul he sailed on a day
    Over the sea to Skye.

Mull was astern, Rum on the port,
    Eigg on the starboard bow;
Glory of youth glowed in his soul:
    Where is that glory now?

Sing me a song of a lad that is gone,
    Say, could that lad be I?
Merry of soul he sailed on a day
    Over the sea to Skye.

Give me again all that was there,

    Give me the sun that shone !

Give me the eyes, give me the soul,

    Give me the lad that's gone !

Sing me a song of a lad that is gone,

    Say, could that lad be I ?

Merry of soul he sailed on a day

    Over the sea to Skye.

Billow and breeze, islands and seas,

    Mountains of rain and sun,

All that was good, all that was fair,

    All that was me is gone.

TO S. R. CROCKETT

(On receiving a Dedication)

Blows the wind to-day, and the sun and the rain are flying,
    Blows the wind on the moors to-day and now,
Where about the graves of the martyrs the whaups are crying,
    My heart remembers how !

Grey recumbent tombs of the dead in desert places,
    Standing stones on the vacant wine-red moor,
Hills of sheep, and the homes of the silent vanished races,
    And winds, austere and pure :

Be it granted me to behold you again in dying,
    Hills of home ! and to hear again the call ;
Hear about the graves of the martyrs the peewees crying,
    And hear no more at all.

    Vailima.

XLIV

EVENSONG

THE embers of the day are red

Beyond the murky hill.

The kitchen smokes : the bed

In the darkling house is spread :

The great sky darkens overhead,

And the great woods are shrill.

So far have I been led,

Lord, by Thy will :

So far I have followed, Lord, and wondered still.

The breeze from the enbalmèd land

Blows sudden toward the shore,

And claps my cottage door.

I hear the signal, Lord—I understand.

The night at Thy command

Comes.   I will eat and sleep and will not question more.

Vailima.

LIST OF BOOKS PUBLISHED BY
CHATTO & WINDUS
214 PICCADILLY, LONDON, W.

About (Edmond).—The Fellah: An Egyptian Novel. Translated by Sir RANDAL ROBERTS. Post 8vo, illustrated boards, 2s.

Adams (W. Davenport), Works by.
A Dictionary of the Drama: being a comprehensive Guide to the Plays, Playwrights, Players, and Playhouses of the United Kingdom and America, from the Earliest Times to the Present Day. Crown 8vo, half-bound, 12s. 6d. [*Preparing.*
Quips and Quiddities. Selected by W. DAVENPORT ADAMS. Post 8vo, cloth limp, 2s. 6d.

Agony Column (The) of 'The Times,' from 1800 to 1870. Edited, with an Introduction, by ALICE CLAY. Post 8vo, cloth limp, 2s. 6d.

Aidé (Hamilton), Novels by. Post 8vo, illustrated boards, 2s. each.
Carr of Carrlyon. | **Confidences.**

Albert (Mary).—Brooke Finchley's Daughter. Post 8vo, picture boards, 2s.; cloth limp, 2s. 6d.

Alden (W. L.).—A Lost Soul: Being the Confession and Defence of Charles Lindsay. Fcap. 8vo, cloth boards, 1s. 6d.

Alexander (Mrs.), Novels by. Post 8vo, illustrated boards, 2s. each.
Maid, Wife, or Widow? | **Valerie's Fate.**

Allen (F. M.).—Green as Grass. With a Frontispiece. Crown 8vo, cloth, 3s. 6d.

Allen (Grant), Works by.
The Evolutionist at Large. Crown 8vo, cloth extra, 6s.
Post-Prandial Philosophy. Crown 8vo, art linen, 3s. 6d.
Moorland Idylls. Crown 8vo, cloth decorated, 6s.

Crown 8vo, cloth extra, 3s. 6d. each; post 8vo, illustrated boards, 2s. each.

Philistia.	**In all Shades.**	**Dumaresq's Daughter.**
Babylon. 12 Illustrations.	**The Devil's Die.**	**The Duchess of Powysland**
Strange Stories. Frontis.	**This Mortal Coil.**	**Blood Royal.**
The Beckoning Hand.	**The Tents of Shem.** Frontis.	**Ivan Greet's Masterpiece.**
For Maimie's Sake.	**The Great Taboo.**	**The Scallywag.** 24 Illusts.

Crown 8vo, cloth extra, 3s. 6d. each.

At Market Value. | **Under Sealed Orders.**

Dr. Palliser's Patient. Fcap. 8vo, cloth boards, 1s. 6d.

Anderson (Mary).—Othello's Occupation: A Novel. Crown 8vo, cloth, 3s. 6d.

Arnold (Edwin Lester), Stories by.
The Wonderful Adventures of Phra the Phœnician. Crown 8vo, cloth extra, with 12 Illustrations by H. M. PAGET, 3s. 6d.; post 8vo, illustrated boards, 2s.
The Constable of St. Nicholas. With Frontispiece by S. L. WOOD. Crown 8vo, cloth, 3s. 6d.

Artemus Ward's Works. With Portrait and Facsimile. Crown 8vo, cloth extra, 7s. 6d.—Also a POPULAR EDITION, post 8vo, picture boards, 2s.
The Genial Showman: The Life and Adventures of ARTEMUS WARD. By EDWARD P. HINGSTON. With a Frontispiece. Crown 8vo, cloth extra, 3s. 6d.

Ashton (John), Works by. Crown 8vo, cloth extra, 7s. 6d. each.

History of the Chap-Books of the 18th Century. With 334 Illustrations.
Social Life in the Reign of Queen Anne. With 85 Illustrations.
Humour, Wit, and Satire of the Seventeenth Century. With 82 Illustrations.
English Caricature and Satire on Napoleon the First. With 115 Illustrations.
Modern Street Ballads. With 57 Illustrations.

Bacteria, Yeast Fungi, and Allied Species, A Synopsis of. By
W. B. GROVE, B A. With 87 Illustrations. Crown 8vo, cloth extra, 3s. 6d.

Bardsley (Rev. C. Wareing, M.A.), Works by.
English Surnames: Their Sources and Significations. Crown 8vo, cloth, 7s. 6d.
Curiosities of Puritan Nomenclature. Crown 8vo, cloth extra, 6s.

Baring Gould (Sabine, Author of 'John Herring,' &c.), Novels by.
Crown 8vo, cloth extra, 3s. 6d. each; post 8vo, illustrated boards, 2s. each.
Red Spider. | Eve.

Barr (Robert: Luke Sharp), Stories by. Cr. 8vo, cl., 3s. 6d. each
In a Steamer Chair. With Frontispiece and Vignette by DEMAIN HAMMOND.
From Whose Bourne, &c, With 47 Illustrations by HAL HURST and others.

A Woman Intervenes. With 8 Illustrations by HAL HURST. Crown 8vo, cloth extra, 6s.
Revenge! With 12 Illustrations by LANCELOT SPEED, &c. Crown 8vo, cloth, 6s.   [Shortly

Barrett (Frank), Novels by.
Post 8vo, illustrated boards, 2s. each; cloth, 2s. 6d. each.

Fettered for Life.	A Prodigal's Progress.
The Sin of Olga Zassoulich.	John Ford; and His Helpmate.
Between Life and Death.	A Recoiling Vengeance.
Folly Morrison.	Honest Davie.	Lieut. Barnabas.	Found Guilty.
Little Lady Linton.	For Love and Honour.

The Woman of the Iron Bracelets. Cr. 8vo. cloth, 3s. 6d.; post 8vo, boards, 2s.; cl. limp, 2s. 6d
The Harding Scandal. 2 vols., 10s. net.

Barrett (Joan).—Monte Carlo Stories. Fcap. 8vo, cloth, 1s. 6d.

Beaconsfield, Lord. By T. P. O'CONNOR, M.P. Cr. 8vo, cloth, 5s.

Beauchamp (Shelsley).—Grantley Grange. Post 8vo, boards, 2s.

Beautiful Pictures by British Artists: A Gathering of Favourites
from the Picture Galleries, engraved on Steel. Imperial 4to, cloth extra, gilt edges, 21s.

Besant (Sir Walter) and James Rice, Novels by.
Crown 8vo, cloth extra, 3s. 6d. each; post 8vo, illustrated boards, 2s. each; cloth limp, 2s. 6d. each.

Ready-Money Mortiboy.	By Celia's Arbour.
My Little Girl.	The Chaplain of the Fleet.
With Harp and Crown.	The Seamy Side.
This Son of Vulcan.	The Case of Mr. Lucraft, &c.
The Golden Butterfly.	'Twas in Trafalgar's Bay, &c.
The Monks of Thelema.	The Ten Years' Tenant, &c.

** There is also a LIBRARY EDITION of the above Twelve Volumes, handsomely set in new type on a large crown 8vo page, and bound in cloth extra, 6s. each; and a POPULAR EDITION of **The Golden Butterfly,** medium 8vo, 6d.; cloth, 1s.—NEW EDITIONS, printed in large type on crown 8vo laid paper, bound in figured cloth, 3s. 6d. each, are also in course of publication.

Besant (Sir Walter), Novels by.
Crown 8vo, cloth extra, 3s. 6d. each; post 8vo, illustrated boards, 2s. each; cloth limp, 2s. 6d. each.
All Sorts and Conditions of Men. With 12 Illustrations by FRED. BARNARD
The Captains' Room, &c. With Frontispiece by E. J. WHEELER.
All in a Garden Fair. With 6 Illustrations by HARRY FURNISS.
Dorothy Forster. With Frontispiece by CHARLES GREEN.
Uncle Jack, and other Stories. | **Children of Gibeon.**
The World Went Very Well Then. With 12 Illustrations by A. FORESTIER.
Herr Paulus: His Rise, his Greatness, and his Fall. | **The Bell of St. Paul's.**
For Faith and Freedom. With Illustrations by A. FORESTIER and F. WADDY.
To Call Her Mine, &c. With 9 Illustrations by A. FORESTIER.
The Holy Rose, &c. With Frontispiece by F. BARNARD.
Armorel of Lyonesse: A Romance of To-day. With 12 Illustrations by F. BARNARD.
St. Katherine's by the Tower. With 12 Illustrations by C. GREEN.
Verbena Camellia Stephanotis, &c. With a Frontispiece by GORDON BROWNE.
The Ivory Gate. | **The Rebel Queen.**

Beyond the Dreams of Avarice. With 12 Illusts. by W. H. HYDE. Crown 8vo, cloth extra, 3s. 6d.
In Deacon's Orders, &c. With Frontispiece by A. FORESTIER. Crown 8vo, cloth, 6s.
The Master Craftsman. 2 vols., crown 8vo, 10s. net. SECOND EDITION.

Fifty Years Ago. With 144 Plates and Woodcuts. Crown 8vo, cloth extra, 5s.
The Eulogy of Richard Jefferies. With Portrait. Crown 8vo, cloth extra, 6s.
London. With 125 Illustrations. Demy 8vo, cloth extra, 7s. 6d.
Westminster. With Etched Frontispiece by F. S. WALKER, R.P.E., and 130 Illustrations by WILLIAM PATTEN and others. Demy 8vo, cloth, 18s.
Sir Richard Whittington. With Frontispiece. Crown 8vo, art linen, 3s. 6d.
Gaspard de Coligny. With a Portrait. Crown 8vo, art linen, 3s. 6d.
As we Are: As we May Be: Social Essays. Crown 8vo, linen, 6s.   [Shortly.

Bechstein (Ludwig).—As Pretty as Seven, and other German Stories. With Additional Tales by the Brothers GRIMM, and 98 Illustrations by RICHTER. Square 8vo, cloth extra, 6s. 6d.: gilt edges, 7s. 6d.

Beerbohm (Julius).—Wanderings in Patagonia; or, Life among the Ostrich-Hunters. With Illustrations. Crown 8vo, cloth extra, 3s. 6d.

Bellew (Frank).—The Art of Amusing: A Collection of Graceful Arts, Games, Tricks, Puzzles, and Charades. With 300 Illustrations. Crown 8vo, cloth extra, 4s. 6d.

Bennett (W. C., LL.D.).—Songs for Sailors. Post 8vo, cl. limp, 2s.

Bewick (Thomas) and his Pupils. By AUSTIN DOBSON. With 95 Illustrations. Square 8vo, cloth extra, 6s.

Bierce (Ambrose).—In the Midst of Life: Tales of Soldiers and Civilians. Crown 8vo, cloth extra, 6s.; post 8vo, illustrated boards, 2s.

Bill Nye's History of the United States. With 146 Illustrations by F. OPPER. Crown 8vo, cloth extra, 3s. 6d.

Biré (Edmond). — Diary of a Citizen of Paris during 'The Terror.' Translated and Edited by JOHN DE VILLIERS. With 2 Photogravures. Two Vols., demy 8vo, cloth, 21s. [Shortly.

Blackburn's (Henry) Art Handbooks.

Academy Notes, 1875, 1877-86, 1889, 1890, 1892-1895, Illustrated, each 1s.
Academy Notes, 1896. 1s.
Academy Notes, 1875-79. Complete in One Vol., with 600 Illustrations. Cloth, 6s.
Academy Notes, 1880-84. Complete in One Vol., with 700 Illustrations. Cloth, 6s.
Academy Notes, 1890-94. Complete in One Vol., with 800 Illustrations. Cloth, 7s. 6d.
Grosvenor Notes, 1877. 6d.
Grosvenor Notes, separate years from 1878-1890, each 1s.
Grosvenor Notes, Vol. I., 1877-82. With 300 Illustrations. Demy 8vo, cloth, 6s.

Grosvenor Notes, Vol. II., 1883-87. With 300 Illustrations. Demy 8vo, cloth, 6s.
Grosvenor Notes, Vol. III., 1889-90. With 230 Illustrations. Demy 8vo cloth, 3s. 6d.
The New Gallery, 1888-1895. With numerous Illustrations, each 1s.
The New Gallery, Vol. I., 1888-1892. With 250 Illustrations. Demy 8vo, cloth, 6s.
English Pictures at the National Gallery. With 114 Illustrations. 1s.
Old Masters at the National Gallery. With 128 Illustrations. 1s. 6d.
Illustrated Catalogue to the National Gallery. With 242 Illusts. Demy 8vo, cloth, 3s.

The Illustrated Catalogue of the Paris Salon, 1896. With 300 Facsimile Sketches. 3s.

Blind (Mathilde), Poems by.
The Ascent of Man. Crown 8vo, cloth, 5s.
Dramas in Miniature. With a Frontispiece by F. MADOX BROWN. Crown 8vo, cloth, 5s.
Songs and Sonnets. Fcap. 8vo, vellum and gold, 5s.
Birds of Passage: Songs of the Orient and Occident. Second Edition. Crown 8vo, linen, 6s. net.

Bourget (Paul).—A Living Lie. Translated by JOHN DE VILLIERS. With special Preface for the English Edition. Crown 8vo, cloth, 3s. 6d.

Bourne (H. R. Fox), Books by.
English Merchants: Memoirs in Illustration of the Progress of British Commerce. With numerous Illustrations. Crown 8vo, cloth extra, 7s. 6d.
English Newspapers: Chapters in the History of Journalism. Two Vols., demy 8vo, cloth, 25s.
The Other Side of the Emin Pasha Relief Expedition. Crown 8vo, cloth, 6s.

Bowers (George).—Leaves from a Hunting Journal. Coloured Plates. Oblong folio, half-bound, 21s.

Boyle (Frederick), Works by. Post 8vo, illustrated bds., 2s. each.
Chronicles of No-Man's Land. | Camp Notes. | Savage Life.

Brand (John).—Observations on Popular Antiquities; chiefly illustrating the Origin of our Vulgar Customs, Ceremonies, and Superstitions. With the Additions of Sir HENRY ELLIS, and numerous Illustrations. Crown 8vo, cloth extra, 7s. 6d.

Brewer (Rev. Dr.), Works by.
The Reader's Handbook of Allusions, References, Plots, and Stories. Seventeenth Thousand. Crown 8vo, cloth extra, 7s. 6d.
Authors and their Works, with the Dates: Being the Appendices to 'The Reader's Handbook,' separately printed. Crown 8vo, cloth limp, 2s.
A Dictionary of Miracles. Crown 8vo, cloth extra, 7s. 6d.

Brewster (Sir David), Works by. Post 8vo, cloth, 4s. 6d. each.
More Worlds than One: Creed of the Philosopher and Hope of the Christian. With Plates.
The Martyrs of Science: GALILEO, TYCHO BRAHE, and KEPLER. With Portraits.
Letters on Natural Magic. With numerous Illustrations.

Brillat-Savarin.—Gastronomy as a Fine Art. Translated by R. E. ANDERSON, M.A. Post 8vo, half-bound, 2s.

Brydges (Harold).—Uncle Sam at Home. With 91 Illustrations. Post 8vo, illustrated boards, 2s.; cloth limp, 2s. 6d.

Buchanan (Robert), Novels, &c., by.

Crown 8vo, cloth extra, 3s. 6d. each; pos 8vo, illustrated boards, 2s. each.

The Shadow of the Sword.
A Child of Nature. With Frontispiece.
God and the Man. With 11 Illustrations by FRED. BARNARD.
The Martyrdom of Madeline. With Frontispiece by A. W. COOPER.

Love Me for Ever. With Frontispiece.
Annan Water. | **Foxglove Manor.**
The New Abelard.
Matt: A Story of a Caravan. With Frontispiece.
The Master of the Mine. With Frontispiece
The Heir of Linne. | **Woman and the Man**

Crown 8vo, cloth extra, 3s. 6d. each.

Red and White Heather. | **Rachel Dene.**

Lady Kilpatrick. Crown 8vo, cloth extra, 6s.
The Wandering Jew: a Christmas Carol. Crown 8vo, cloth, 6s,

The Charlatan. By ROBERT BUCHANAN and HENRY MURRAY. With a Frontispiece by T. H ROBINSON. Crown 8vo, cloth, 3s. 6d.

Burton (Richard F.).—The Book of the Sword. With over 400

Illustrations. Demy 4to, cloth extra, 32s.

Burton (Robert).—The Anatomy of Melancholy. With Transla

tions of the Quotations. Demy 8vo, cloth extra, 7s. 6d.
Melancholy Anatomised: An Abridgment of BURTON'S ANATOMY. Post 8vo, half-bd., 2s. 6d

Caine (T. Hall), Novels by. Crown 8vo, cloth extra, 3s. 6d. each.

post 8vo, illustrated boards, 2s. each; cloth limp, 2s. 6d. each.

The Shadow of a Crime. | **A Son of Hagar.** | **The Deemster.**
A LIBRARY EDITION OF **The Deemster** is now ready; and one of **The Shadow of a Crim** is in preparation, set in new type, crown 8vo, cloth decorated, 6s. each.

Cameron (Commander V. Lovett).—The Cruise of the 'Black

Prince' Privateer. Post 8vo, picture boards, 2s.

Cameron (Mrs. H. Lovett), Novels by. Post 8vo, illust. bds. 2s. ea

Juliet's Guardian. | **Deceivers Ever.**

Carlyle (Jane Welsh), Life of. By Mrs. ALEXANDER IRELAND. With

Portrait and Facsimile Letter. Small demy 8vo, cloth extra, 7s. 6d.

Carlyle (Thomas).—On the Choice of Books. Post 8vo, cl., 1s. 6d

Correspondence of Thomas Carlyle and R. W. Emerson, 1834-1872. Edited by C. E. NORTON. With Portraits. Two Vols., crown 8vo, cloth, 24s.

Carruth (Hayden).—The Adventures of Jones. With 17 Illustra

tions. Fcap. 8vo, cloth, 2s.

Chambers (Robert W.), Stories of Paris Life by. Long fcap. 8vo

cloth, 2s. 6d. each.
The King in Yellow. | **In the Quarter.**

Chapman's (George), Works. Vol. I., Plays Complete, including the

Doubtful Ones.—Vol. II., Poems and Minor Translations, with Essay by A. C. SWINBURNE.—Vol III., Translations of the Iliad and Odyssey. Three Vols., crown 8vo, cloth, 6s. each.

Chapple (J. Mitchell).—The Minor Chord: The Story of a Prima

Donna. Crown 8vo, cloth, 3s. 6d.

Chatto (W. A.) and J. Jackson.—A Treatise on Wood Engraving

Historical and Practical. With Chapter by H. G. BOHN, and 450 fine Illusts. Large 4to, half-leather, 28s.

Chaucer for Children: A Golden Key. By Mrs. H. R. HAWEIS. With

8 Coloured Plates and 30 Woodcuts. Crown 4to, cloth extra, 3s. 6d.
Chaucer for Schools. By Mrs. H. R. HAWEIS. Demy 8vo, cloth limp, 2s. 6d,

Chess, The Laws and Practice of. With an Analysis of the Open-

ings. By HOWARD STAUNTON. Edited by R. B. WORMALD. Crown 8vo, cloth, 5s.
The Minor Tactics of Chess: A Treatise on the Deployment of the Forces in obedience to Strategic Principle. By F. K. YOUNG and E. C. HOWELL. Long fcap. 8vo, cloth, 2s. 6d.
The Hastings Chess Tournament, 1895. Containing the Authorised Account of the 230 Games played Aug.-Sept., 1895. With Annotations by PILLSBURY, LASKER, TARRASCH, STEI NITZ, SCHIFFERS, TEICHMANN, BARDELEBEN, BLACKBURNE, GUNSBERG, TINSLEY, MASON and ALBIN; and Biographical Sketches of the Chess Masters. Edited by H. F. CHESHIRE. With Twenty-two Portraits. Crown 8vo, cloth, 7s. 6d. net.

Clare (Austin).—For the Love of a Lass. Post 8vo, 2s.; cl., 2s. 6d.

Clive (Mrs. Archer), Novels by. Post 8vo, illust. boards, 2s. each.

Paul Ferroll. | **Why Paul Ferroll Killed his Wife.**

Clodd (Edward, F.R.A.S.).—Myths and Dreams. Cr. 8vo, 3s. 6d.

Cobban (J. Maclaren), Novels by.
The Cure of Souls. Post 8vo, Illustrated boards, 2s.
The Red Sultan. Crown 8vo, cloth extra, 3s. 6d. ; post 8vo, illustrated boards, 2s.
The Burden of Isabel. Crown 8vo, cloth extra, 3s. 6d.

Coleman (John).—Players and Playwrights I have Known. Two
Vols., demy 8vo, cloth, 24s.

Coleridge (M. E.).—The Seven Sleepers of Ephesus. Cloth, 1s. 6d.

Collins (C. Allston).—The Bar Sinister. Post 8vo, boards, 2s.

Collins (John Churton, M.A.), Books by.
Illustrations of Tennyson. Crown 8vo, cloth extra, 6s.
Jonathan Swift: A Biographical and Critical Study. Crown 8vo, cloth extra, 8s.

Collins (Mortimer and Frances), Novels by.
Crown 8vo, cloth extra, 3s. 6d. each ; post 8vo, illustrated boards, 2s. each.
From Midnight to Midnight. | Blacksmith and Scholar.
Transmigration. | You Play me False. | A Village Comedy.
Post 8vo, illustrated boards, 2s. each.
Sweet Anne Page. | A Fight with Fortune. | Sweet and Twenty. | Frances

Collins (Wilkie), Novels by.
Crown 8vo, cloth extra, 3s. 6d. each ; post 8vo, illustrated boards, 2s. each ; cloth limp, 2s. 6d. each.
Antonina. With a Frontispiece by Sir JOHN GILBERT, R.A.
Basil. Illustrated by Sir JOHN GILBERT, R.A., and J. MAHONEY.
Hide and Seek. Illustrated by Sir JOHN GILBERT, R.A., and J. MAHONEY.
After Dark. With Illustrations by A. B. HOUGHTON. | The Two Destinies.
The Dead Secret. With a Frontispiece by Sir JOHN GILBERT, R.A.
Queen of Hearts. With a Frontispiece by Sir JOHN GILBERT, R.A.
The Woman in White. With Illustrations by Sir JOHN GILBERT, R.A., and F. A. FRASER.
No Name. With Illustrations by Sir J. E. MILLAIS, R.A., and A. W. COOPER.
My Miscellanies. With a Steel-plate Portrait of WILKIE COLLINS.
Armadale. With Illustrations by G. H. THOMAS.
The Moonstone. With Illustrations by G. DU MAURIER and F. A. FRASER.
Man and Wife. With Illustrations by WILLIAM SMALL.
Poor Miss Finch. Illustrated by G. DU MAURIER and EDWARD HUGHES.
Miss or Mrs.? With Illustrations by S. L. FILDES, R.A., and HENRY WOODS, A.R.A.
The New Magdalen. Illustrated by G. DU MAURIER and C. S. REINHARDT.
The Frozen Deep. Illustrated by G. DU MAURIER and J. MAHONEY.
The Law and the Lady. With Illustrations by S. L. FILDES, R.A., and SYDNEY HALL.
The Haunted Hotel. With Illustrations by ARTHUR HOPKINS.
The Fallen Leaves. | Heart and Science. | The Evil Genius.
Jezebel's Daughter. | 'I Say No.' | Little Novels. Frontis.
The Black Robe. | A Rogue's Life. | The Legacy of Cain.
Blind Love. With a Preface by Sir WALTER BESANT, and Illustrations by A. FORESTIER.

POPULAR EDITIONS. Medium 8vo, 6d. each ; cloth, 1s. each.
The Woman in White. | The Moonstone.

The Woman in White and The Moonstone in One Volume, medium 8vo, cloth, 2s.

Colman's (George) Humorous Works: 'Broad Grins,' 'My Night-
gown and Slippers,' &c. With Life and Frontispiece. Crown 8vo, cloth extra, 7s. 6d.

Colquhoun (M. J.).—Every Inch a Soldier. Post 8vo, boards, 2s.

Colt-breaking, Hints on. By W. M. HUTCHISON. Cr. 8vo, cl., 3s. 6d.

Convalescent Cookery. By CATHERINE RYAN. Cr. 8vo, 1s. ; cl., 1s. 6d.

Conway (Moncure D.), Works by.
Demonology and Devil-Lore. With 65 Illustrations. Two Vols., demy 8vo, cloth, 28s.
George Washington's Rules of Civility. Fcap. 8vo, Japanese vellum, 2s. 6d.

Cook (Dutton), Novels by.
Paul Foster's Daughter. Crown 8vo, cloth extra, 3s. 6d. ; post 8vo, illustrated boards, 2s.
Leo. Post 8vo, illustrated boards, 2s.

Cooper (Edward H.).—Geoffory Hamilton. Cr. 8vo, cloth. 3s. 6d.

Cornwall.—Popular Romances of the West of England; or, The
Drolls, Traditions, and Superstitions of Old Cornwall. Collected by ROBERT HUNT, F.R.S. With
two Steel Plates by GEORGE CRUIKSHANK. Crown 8vo, cloth, 7s. 6d.

Cotes (V. Cecil).—Two Girls on a Barge. With 44 Illustrations by
F. H. TOWNSEND. Post 8vo, cloth, 2s. 6d.

Craddock (C. Egbert), Stories by.
The Prophet of the Great Smoky Mountains. Post 8vo, illustrated boards, 2s.
His Vanished Star. Crown 8vo, cloth extra, 3s. 6d.

Cram (Ralph Adams).—Black Spirits and White. Fcap. 8vo, cloth 1s. 6d.

Crellin (H. N.) Books by.
Romances of the Old Seraglio. With 28 Illustrations by S. L. WOOD. Crown 8vo, cloth, 3s. 6d
Tales of the Caliph. Crown 8vo, cloth, 2s.
The Nazarenes: A Drama. Crown 8vo, 1s.

Crim (Matt.).—Adventures of a Fair Rebel. Crown 8vo, cloth extra, with a Frontispiece by DAN. BEARD, 3s. 6d.; post 8vo, illustrated boards, 2s.

Crockett (S. R.) and others.—Tales of Our Coast. By S. R CROCKETT, GILBERT PARKER, HAROLD FREDERIC, 'Q.,' and W CLARK RUSSELL. With 12 Illustrations by FRANK BRANGWYN. Crown 8vo, cloth, 3s. 6d.

Croker (Mrs. B. M.), Novels by. Crown 8vo, cloth extra, 3s. 6d. each; post 8vo, illustrated boards 2s. each; cloth limp, 2s. 6d. each.

Pretty Miss Neville.	Diana Barrington.	A Family Likeness.
A Bird of Passage.	Proper Pride.	'To Let.'

Village Tales and Jungle Tragedies.
Crown 8vo, cloth extra, 3s. 6d. each.

Mr. Jervis.	The Real Lady Hilda.

Married or Single? Three Vols., crown 8vo, 15s. net.

Cruikshank's Comic Almanack. Complete in Two SERIES: The FIRST, from 1835 to 1843; the SECOND, from 1844 to 1853. A Gathering of the Best Humour of THACKERAY, HOOD, MAYHEW, ALBERT SMITH, A'BECKETT, ROBERT BROUGH, &c. With numerous Steel Engravings and Woodcuts by GEORGE CRUIKSHANK, HINE, LANDELLS, &c. Two Vols., crown 8vo, cloth gilt, 7s. 6d. each.
The Life of George Cruikshank. By BLANCHARD JERROLD. With 84 Illustrations and a Bibliography. Crown 8vo, cloth extra, 6s.

Cumming (C. F. Gordon), Works by. Demy 8vo, cl. ex., 8s. 6d. ea.
In the Hebrides. With an Autotype Frontispiece and 23 Illustrations.
In the Himalayas and on the Indian Plains. With 42 Illustrations.
Two Happy Years in Ceylon. With 28 Illustrations.
Via Cornwall to Egypt. With a Photogravure Frontispiece. Demy 8vo, cloth, 7s. 6d.

Cussans (John E.).—A Handbook of Heraldry; with Instructions for Tracing Pedigrees and Deciphering Ancient MSS., &c. Fourth Edition, revised, with 408 Woodcuts and 2 Coloured Plates. Crown 8vo, cloth extra, 6s.

Cyples (W.).—Hearts of Gold. Cr. 8vo, cl., 3s. 6d.; post 8vo, bds., 2s.

Daniel (George).—Merrie England in the Olden Time. With Illustrations by ROBERT CRUIKSHANK. Crown 8vo, cloth extra, 3s. 6d.

Daudet (Alphonse).—The Evangelist; or, Port Salvation. Crown 8vo, cloth extra, 3s. 6d.; post 8vo, illustrated boards, 2s.

Davenant (Francis, M.A.).—Hints for Parents on the Choice of a Profession for their Sons when Starting in Life. Crown 8vo, 1s.; cloth, 1s. 6d.

Davidson (Hugh Coleman).—Mr. Sadler's Daughters. With a Frontispiece by STANLEY WOOD. Crown 8vo, cloth extra, 3s. 6d.

Davies (Dr. N. E. Yorke-), Works by. Cr. 8vo, 1s. ea.; cl., 1s. 6d. ea.
One Thousand Medical Maxims and Surgical Hints.
Nursery Hints: A Mother's Guide in Health and Disease.
Foods for the Fat: A Treatise on Corpulency, and a Dietary for its Cure.
Aids to Long Life. Crown 8vo, 2s.; cloth limp, 2s. 6d.

Davies' (Sir John) Complete Poetical Works. Collected and Edited, with Introduction and Notes, by Rev. A. B. GROSART, D.D. Two Vols., crown 8vo, cloth, 12s.

Dawson (Erasmus, M.B.).—The Fountain of Youth. Crown 8vo, cloth extra, with Two Illustrations by HUME NISBET, 3s. 6d.; post 8vo, illustrated boards, 2s.

De Guerin (Maurice), The Journal of. Edited by G. S. TREBUTIEN. With a Memoir by SAINTE-BEUVE. Translated from the 20th French Edition by JESSIE P. FROTH INGHAM. Fcap. 8vo, half-bound, 2s. 6d.

De Maistre (Xavier).—A Journey Round my Room. Translated by Sir HENRY ATTWELL. Post 8vo, cloth limp, 2s. 6d.

De Mille (James).—A Castle in Spain. Crown 8vo, cloth extra, with a Frontispiece, 3s. 6d.; post 8vo, illustrated boards, 2s.

Derby (The): The Blue Ribbon of the Turf. With Brief Accounts of THE OAKS. By LOUIS HENRY CURZON. Crown 8vo, cloth limp, 2s. 6d.

Derwent (Leith), Novels by. Cr. 8vo, cl., 3s. 6d. ea.; post 8vo, 2s. ea.
Our Lady of Tears. | Circe's Lovers.

Dewar (T. R.).—A Ramble Round the Globe. With 220 Illustrations. Crown 8vo, cloth extra, 7s. 6d.

Dickens (Charles), Novels by. Post 8vo, illustrated boards, 2s. each.
Sketches by Boz. | Nicholas Nickleby. | Oliver Twist.

About England with Dickens. By ALFRED RIMMER. With 57 Illustrations by C. A. VANDER-HOOF, ALFRED RIMMER, and others. Square 8vo, cloth extra, 7s. 6d.

Dictionaries.
A Dictionary of Miracles: Imitative, Realistic, and Dogmatic. By the Rev. E. C. BREWER, LL.D. Crown 8vo, cloth extra, 7s. 6d.
The Reader's Handbook of Allusions, References, Plots, and Stories. By the Rev. E. C. BREWER, LL.D. With an ENGLISH BIBLIOGRAPHY. Crown 8vo, cloth extra, 7s. 6d.
Authors and their Works, with the Dates. Crown 8vo, cloth limp, 2s.
Familiar Short Sayings of Great Men. With Historical and Explanatory Notes by SAMUEL A. BENT, A.M. Crown 8vo, cloth extra, 7s. 6d.
The Slang Dictionary: Etymological, Historical, and Anecdotal. Crown 8vo, cloth, 6s. 6d.
Words, Facts, and Phrases: A Dictionary of Curious, Quaint, and Out-of-the-Way Matters. By ELIEZER EDWARDS. Crown 8vo, cloth extra, 7s. 6d.

Diderot.—The Paradox of Acting. Translated, with Notes, by WALTER HERRIES POLLOCK. With Preface by Sir HENRY IRVING. Crown 8vo, parchment, 4s. 6d.

Dobson (Austin), Works by.
Thomas Bewick and his Pupils. With 95 Illustrations. Square 8vo, cloth, 6s.
Four Frenchwomen. With Four Portraits. Crown 8vo, buckram, gilt top, 6s.
Eighteenth Century Vignettes. TWO SERIES Crown 8vo, buckram, 6s. each.—A THIRD SERIES is in preparation.

Dobson (W. T.).—Poetical Ingenuities and Eccentricities. Post 8vo, cloth limp, 2s. 6d.

Donovan (Dick), Detective Stories by.
Post 8vo, illustrated boards, 2s. each; cloth limp, 2s. 6d. each.

The Man-Hunter. | Wanted.
Caught at Last.
Tracked and Taken.
Who Poisoned Hetty Duncan?
Suspicion Aroused.

A Detective's Triumphs.
In the Grip of the Law.
From Information Received.
Link by Link. | Dark Deeds.
Riddles Read.

Crown 8vo, cloth extra, 3s. 6d. each; post 8vo, illustrated boards, 2s. each; cloth, 2s. 6d. each.
The Man from Manchester. With 23 Illustrations.
Tracked to Doom. With Six full-page Illustrations by GORDON BROWNE.

The Mystery of Jamaica Terrace. Crown 8vo, cloth, 3s. 6d.

Doyle (A. Conan).—The Firm of Girdlestone. Cr. 8vo, cl., 3s. 6d.

Dramatists, The Old. Crown 8vo, cl. ex., with Portraits, 6s. per Vol.
Ben Jonson's Works. With Notes, Critical and Explanatory, and a Biographical Memoir by WILLIAM GIFFORD. Edited by Colonel CUNNINGHAM. Three Vols.
Chapman's Works. Three Vols. Vol. I. contains the Plays complete; Vol. II., Poems and Minor Translations, with an Essay by A. C. SWINBURNE; Vol. III., Translations of the Iliad and Odyssey.
Marlowe's Works. Edited, with Notes, by Colonel CUNNINGHAM. One Vol.
Massinger's Plays. From GIFFORD'S Text. Edited by Colonel CUNNINGHAM. One Vol.

Duncan (Sara Jeannette: Mrs. EVERARD COTES), Works by.
Crown 8vo, cloth extra, 7s. 6d. each.
A Social Departure. With 111 Illustrations by F. H. TOWNSEND.
An American Girl in London. With 80 Illustrations by F. H. TOWNSEND.
The Simple Adventures of a Memsahib. With 37 Illustrations by F. H. TOWNSEND.

Crown 8vo, cloth extra, 3s. 6d. each.
A Daughter of To-Day. | Vernon's Aunt. With 47 Illustrations by HAL HURST.

Dyer (T. F. Thiselton).—The Folk=Lore of Plants. Cr. 8vo, cl., 6s.

Early English Poets. Edited, with Introductions and Annotations, by Rev. A. B. GROSART, D.D. Crown 8vo, cloth boards, 6s. per Volume.
Fletcher's (Giles) Complete Poems. One Vol.
Davies' (Sir John) Complete Poetical Works. Two Vols.
Herrick's (Robert) Complete Collected Poems. Three Vols.
Sidney's (Sir Philip) Complete Poetical Works. Three Vols.

Edgcumbe (Sir E. R. Pearce).—Zephyrus: A Holiday in Brazil and on the River Plate. With 41 Illustrations. Crown 8vo, cloth extra, 5s.

Edison, The Life and Inventions of Thomas A. By W. K. L. and ANTONIA DICKSON. With 200 Illustrations by R. F. OUTCALT, &c. Demy 4to, cloth gilt, 18s.

Edwardes (Mrs. Annie), Novels by.
Post 8vo, illustrated boards, 2s. each.

Archie Lovell. | **A Point of Honour.**

Edwards (Eliezer).—Words, Facts, and Phrases: A Dictionary
of Curious Quaint, and Out-of-the-Way Matters. Crown 8vo, cloth, 7s. 6d.

Edwards (M. Betham=), Novels by.
Kitty. Post 8vo, boards, 2s. ; cloth, 2s. 6d. | **Felicia.** Post 8vo, illustrated boards, 2s.

Egerton (Rev. J. C., M.A.). — Sussex Folk and Sussex Ways.
With Introduction by Rev. Dr. H. WACE, and Four Illustrations. Crown 8vo, cloth extra, 5s.

Eggleston (Edward).—Roxy: A Novel. Post 8vo, illust. boards, 2s.

Englishman's House, The: A Practical Guide for Selecting or Build-
ing a House. By C. J. RICHARDSON. Coloured Frontispiece and 534 Illusts. Cr. 8vo, cloth, 7s. 6d.

Ewald (Alex. Charles, F.S.A.), Works by.
The Life and Times of Prince Charles Stuart, Count of Albany (THE YOUNG PRETEN-
DER). With a Portrait. Crown 8vo, cloth extra, 7s. 6d.
Stories from the State Papers. With Autotype Frontispiece. Crown 8vo, cloth, 6s.

Eyes, Our: How to Preserve Them. By JOHN BROWNING. Cr. 8vo, 1s.

Familiar Short Sayings of Great Men. By SAMUEL ARTHUR BENT.
A.M. Fifth Edition, Revised and Enlarged. Crown 8vo, cloth extra, 7s. 6d.

Faraday (Michael), Works by. Post 8vo, cloth extra, 4s. 6d. each.
The Chemical History of a Candle: Lectures delivered before a Juvenile Audience. Edited
by WILLIAM CROOKES, F.C.S. With numerous Illustrations.
On the Various Forces of Nature, and their Relations to each other. Edited by
WILLIAM CROOKES, F.C.S. With Illustrations.

Farrer (J. Anson), Works by.
Military Manners and Customs. Crown 8vo, cloth extra, 6s.
War: Three Essays, reprinted from 'Military Manners and Customs.' Crown 8vo, 1s. ; cloth, 1s. 6d.

Fenn (G. Manville), Novels by.
Crown 8vo, cloth extra, 3s. 6d. each ; post 8vo, illustrated boards, 2s. each.
The New Mistress. | **Witness to the Deed.**
The Tiger Lily: A Tale of Two Passions.

The White Virgin. Crown 8vo, cloth extra, 3s. 6d.

Fin-Bec.—The Cupboard Papers: Observations on the Art of Living
and Dining. Post 8vo, cloth limp, 2s. 6d.

Fireworks, The Complete Art of Making; or, The Pyrotechnist's
Treasury. By THOMAS KENTISH. With 267 Illustrations. Crown 8vo, cloth, 5s.

First Book, My. By WALTER BESANT, JAMES PAYN, W. CLARK RUS-
SELL, GRANT ALLEN, HALL CAINE, GEORGE R. SIMS, RUDYARD KIPLING, A. CONAN DOYLE,
M. E. BRADDON, F. W. ROBINSON, H. RIDER HAGGARD, R. M. BALLANTYNE, I. ZANGWILL,
MORLEY ROBERTS, D. CHRISTIE MURRAY, MARY CORELLI, J. K. JEROME, JOHN STRANGE
WINTER, BRET HARTE, 'Q.,' ROBERT BUCHANAN, and R. L. STEVENSON. With a Prefatory Story
by JEROME K. JEROME, and 185 Illustrations. Small demy 8vo, cloth extra, 7s. 6d.

Fitzgerald (Percy), Works by.
The World Behind the Scenes. Crown 8vo, cloth extra, 3s. 6d.
Little Essays: Passages from the Letters of CHARLES LAMB. Post 8vo, cloth, 2s. 6d.
A Day's Tour: A Journey through France and Belgium. With Sketches. Crown 4to, 1s.
Fatal Zero. Crown 8vo, cloth extra, 3s. 6d. ; post 8vo, illustrated boards, 2s.

Post 8vo, illustrated boards, 2s. each.

Bella Donna. | **The Lady of Brantome.** | **The Second Mrs. Tillotson.**
Polly. | **Never Forgotten.** | **Seventy-five Brooke Street.**

The Life of James Boswell (of Auchinleck). With Illusts. Two Vols., demy 8vo, cloth, 24s.
The Savoy Opera. With 60 Illustrations and Portraits. Crown 8vo, cloth, 3s. 6d.
Sir Henry Irving: Twenty Years at the Lyceum. With Portrait. Crown 8vo, 1s. ; cloth, 1s. 6d.

Flammarion (Camille), Works by.
Popular Astronomy: A General Description of the Heavens. Translated by J. ELLARD GORE,
F.R.A.S. With Three Plates and 288 Illustrations. Medium 8vo, cloth, 16s.
Urania: A Romance. With 87 Illustrations. Crown 8vo, cloth extra, 5s.

Fletcher's (Giles, B.D.) Complete Poems: Christ's Victorie in
Heaven, Christ's Victorie on Earth, Christ's Triumph over Death, and Minor Poems. With Notes by
Rev. A. B. GROSART, D.D. Crown 8vo, cloth boards, 6s.

Fonblanque (Albany).—Filthy Lucre. Post 8vo, illust. boards, 2s.

Francillon (R. E.), Novels by.
Crown 8vo, cloth extra, 3s. 6d. each ; post 8vo, illustrated boards, 2s. each.

One by One. | A Real Queen. | A Dog and his Shadow.
Ropes of Sand. Illustrated.

Post 8vo, illustrated boards, 2s. each.

Queen Cophetua. | Olympia. | Romances of the Law. | King or Knave?

Jack Doyle's Daughter. Crown 8vo, cloth, 3s. 6d.
Esther's Glove. Fcap. 8vo, picture cover, 1s.

Frederic (Harold), Novels by. Post 8vo, illust. boards, 2s. each.
Seth's Brother's Wife. | The Lawton Girl.

French Literature, A History of. By HENRY VAN LAUN. Three
Vols., demy 8vo, cloth boards, 7s. 6d. each.

Friswell (Hain).—One of Two : A Novel. Post 8vo, illust. bds., 2s.

Frost (Thomas), Works by. Crown 8vo, cloth extra, 3s. 6d. each.
Circus Life and Circus Celebrities. | Lives of the Conjurers.
The Old Showmen and the Old London Fairs.

Fry's (Herbert) Royal Guide to the London Charities. Edited
by JOHN LANE. Published Annually. Crown 8vo, cloth, 1s. 6d.

Gardening Books. Post 8vo, 1s. each ; cloth limp. 1s. 6d. each.
A Year's Work in Garden and Greenhouse. By GEORGE GLENNY.
Household Horticulture. By TOM and JANE JERROLD. Illustrated.
The Garden that Paid the Rent. By TOM JERROLD.

My Garden Wild. By FRANCIS G. HEATH. Crown 8vo, cloth extra, 6s.

Gardner (Mrs. Alan).—Rifle and Spear with the Rajpoots : Being
the Narrative of a Winter's Travel and Sport in Northern India. With numerous Illustrations by the
Author and F. H. TOWNSEND. Demy 4to, half-bound, 21s.

Jarrett (Edward).—The Capel Girls: A Novel. Crown 8vo, cloth
extra, with two Illustrations, 3s. 6d. ; post 8vo, illustrated boards, 2s.

Gaulot (Paul).—The Red Shirts: A Story of the Revolution. Translated by JOHN DE VILLIERS. With a Frontispiece by STANLEY WOOD. Crown 8vo, cloth, 3s. 6d.

Gentleman's Magazine, The. 1s. Monthly. Contains Stories,
Articles upon Literature, Science, Biography, and Art, and 'Table Talk' by SYLVANUS URBAN.
*** Bound Volumes for recent years kept in stock, 8s. 6d. each. Cases for binding, 2s.

Gentleman's Annual, The. Published Annually in November. 1s.

German Popular Stories. Collected by the Brothers GRIMM and
Translated by EDGAR TAYLOR. With Introduction by JOHN RUSKIN, and 22 Steel Plates after
GEORGE CRUIKSHANK. Square 8vo, cloth, 6s. 6d. ; gilt edges, 7s. 6d.

Gibbon (Charles), Novels by.
Crown 8vo, cloth extra, 3s. 6d. each ; post 8vo, illustrated boards, 2s. each.

Robin Gray. Frontispiece. | The Golden Shaft. Frontispiece. | Loving a Dream

Post 8vo, illustrated boards, 2s. each.

The Flower of the Forest.
The Dead Heart.
For Lack of Gold.
What Will the World Say?
For the King. | A Hard Knot.
Queen of the Meadow.
In Pastures Green.

In Love and War.
A Heart's Problem.
By Mead and Stream.
The Braes of Yarrow.
Fancy Free. | Of High Degree.
In Honour Bound.
Heart's Delight. | Blood-Money.

Gibney (Somerville).—Sentenced! Crown 8vo, 1s. ; cloth, 1s. 6d.

Gilbert (W. S.), Original Plays by. In Three Series, 2s. 6d. each.
The FIRST SERIES contains : The Wicked World—Pygmalion and Galatea—Charity—The Princess—
The Palace of Truth—Trial by Jury.
The SECOND SERIES : Broken Hearts—Engaged—Sweethearts—Gretchen—Dan'l Druce—Tom Cobb
—H.M.S. 'Pinafore'—The Sorcerer—The Pirates of Penzance.
The THIRD SERIES : Comedy and Tragedy—Foggerty's Fairy—Rosencrantz and Guildenstern—
Patience—Princess Ida—The Mikado—Ruddigore—The Yeomen of the Guard—The Gondoliers—
The Mountebanks—Utopia.

Eight Original Comic Operas written by W. S. GILBERT. Containing : The Sorcerer—H.M.S.
'Pinafore'—The Pirates of Penzance—Iolanthe—Patience—Princess Ida—The Mikado -Trial by
Jury. Demy 8vo, cloth limp, 2s. 6d.

The Gilbert and Sullivan Birthday Book : Quotations for Every Day in the Year, selected
from Plays by W. S. GILBERT set to Music by Sir A. SULLIVAN. Compiled by ALEX. WATSON.
Royal 16mo, Japanese leather, 2s. 6d.

Gilbert (William), Novels by. Post 8vo, illustrated bds., 2s. each.
Dr. Austin's Guests. | James Duke, Costermonger.
The Wizard of the Mountain.

Glanville (Ernest), Novels by.
Crown 8vo, cloth extra, 3s. 6d. each ; post 8vo, illustrated boards, 2s. each.
The Lost Heiress : A Tale of Love, Battle, and Adventure. With Two Illustrations by H. NISBET
The Fossicker : A Romance of Mashonaland. With Two Illustrations by HUME NISBET.
A Fair Colonist. With a Frontispiece by STANLEY WOOD.

The Golden Rock. With a Frontispiece by STANLEY WOOD. Crown 8vo, cloth extra, 3s. 6d.
Kloof Yarns. Crown 8vo, picture cover, 1s. ; cloth, 1s. 6d.

Glenny (George).—A Year's Work in Garden and Greenhouse :
Practical Advice as to the Management of the Flower, Fruit, and Frame Garden. Post 8vo, 1s. ; cloth, 1s. 6d

Godwin (William).—Lives of the Necromancers. Post 8vo, cl., 2s

Golden Treasury of Thought, The : An Encyclopædia of QUOTA-
TIONS. Edited by THEODORE TAYLOR. Crown 8vo, cloth gilt, 7s. 6d.

Gontaut, Memoirs of the Duchesse de (Gouvernante to the Chil-
dren of France), 1773-1836. With Two Photogravures. Two Vols., demy 8vo, cloth extra, 21s.

Goodman (E. J.).—The Fate of Herbert Wayne. Cr. 8vo, 3s. 6d.

Graham (Leonard).—The Professor's Wife : A Story. Fcp. 8vo, 1s.

Greeks and Romans, The Life of the, described from Antique
Monuments. By ERNST GUHL and W. KONER. Edited by Dr. F. HUEFFER. With 545 Illustrations. Large crown 8vo, cloth extra, 7s. 6d.

Greenwood (James), Works by. Crown 8vo, cloth extra, 3s. 6d. each.
The Wilds of London. | Low-Life Deeps.

Greville (Henry), Novels by.
Nikanor. Translated by ELIZA E. CHASE. Post 8vo, illustrated boards, 2s.
A Noble Woman. Crown 8vo, cloth extra, 5s. ; post 8vo, illustrated boards, 2s.

Griffith (Cecil).—Corinthia Marazion : A Novel. Crown 8vo, cloth
extra, 3s. 6d. ; post 8vo, illustrated boards, 2s.

Grundy (Sydney).—The Days of his Vanity : A Passage in the
Life of a Young Man. Crown 8vo, cloth extra, 3s. 6d. ; post 8vo, illustrated boards, 2s.

Habberton (John, Author of ' Helen's Babies '), **Novels by.**
Post 8vo, illustrated boards, 2s. each ; cloth limp, 2s. 6d. each.
Brueton's Bayou. | Country Luck.

Hair, The : Its Treatment in Health, Weakness, and Disease. Translated from the German of Dr. J. PINCUS. Crown 8vo, 1s. ; cloth, 1s. 6d.

Hake (Dr. Thomas Gordon), Poems by. Cr. 8vo, cl. ex., 6s. each.
New Symbols. | Legends of the Morrow. | The Serpent Play.
Maiden Ecstasy. Small 4to, cloth extra, 8s.

Hall (Owen).—The Track of a Storm. Crown 8vo, cloth, 6s.

Hall (Mrs. S. C.).—Sketches of Irish Character. With numerous
Illustrations on Steel and Wood by MACLISE, GILBERT, HARVEY, and GEORGE CRUIKSHANK.
Small demy 8vo, cloth extra, 7s. 6d.

Halliday (Andrew).—Every-day Papers. Post 8vo, boards, 2s.

Handwriting, The Philosophy of. With over 100 Facsimiles and
Explanatory Text. By DON FELIX DE SALAMANCA. Post 8vo, cloth limp, 2s. 6d.

Hanky-Panky : Easy and Difficult Tricks, White Magic, Sleight of
Hand, &c. Edited by W. H. CREMER. With 200 Illustrations. Crown 8vo, cloth extra, 4s. 6d.

Hardy (Lady Duffus).—Paul Wynter's Sacrifice. Post 8vo, bds., 2s.

Hardy (Thomas).—Under the Greenwood Tree. Crown 8vo, cloth
extra, with Portrait and 15 Illustrations, 3s. 6d. ; post 8vo, illustrated boards, 2s. cloth limp, 2s. 6d.

Harper (Charles G.), Works by. Demy 8vo, cloth extra, 16s. each.
The Brighton Road. With Photogravure Frontispiece and 90 Illustrations.
From Paddington to Penzance : The Record of a Summer Tramp. With 105 Illustrations.

Harwood (J. Berwick).—The Tenth Earl. Post 8vo, boards, 2s.

Harte's (Bret) Collected Works. Revised by the Author. LIBRARY EDITION, in Eight Volumes, crown 8vo, cloth extra, 6s. each.
Vol. I. COMPLETE POETICAL AND DRAMATIC WORKS. With Steel-plate Portrait.
,, II. THE LUCK OF ROARING CAMP—BOHEMIAN PAPERS—AMERICAN LEGENDS.
,, III. TALES OF THE ARGONAUTS—EASTERN SKETCHES.
,, IV. GABRIEL CONROY. | Vol. V. STORIES—CONDENSED NOVELS, &c.
,, VI. TALES OF THE PACIFIC SLOPE.
,, VII. TALES OF THE PACIFIC SLOPE—II. With Portrait by JOHN PETTIE, R.A.
,, VIII. TALES OF THE PINE AND THE CYPRESS.

The Select Works of Bret Harte, in Prose and Poetry. With Introductory Essay by J. M. BELLEW, Portrait of the Author, and 50 Illustrations. Crown 8vo, cloth extra, 7s. 6d.
Bret Harte's Poetical Works. Printed on hand-made paper. Crown 8vo, buckram, 4s. 6d.
The Queen of the Pirate Isle. With 28 Original Drawings by KATE GREENAWAY, reproduced in Colours by EDMUND EVANS. Small 4to, cloth, 5s.

Crown 8vo, cloth extra, 3s. 6d. each; post 8vo, picture boards, 2s. each.
A Waif of the Plains. With 60 Illustrations by STANLEY L. WOOD.
A Ward of the Golden Gate. With 59 Illustrations by STANLEY L. WOOD.

Crown 8vo, cloth extra, 3s. 6d. each.
A Sappho of Green Springs, &c. With Two Illustrations by HUME NISBET.
Colonel Starbottle's Client, and Some Other People. With a Frontispiece.
Susy: A Novel. With Frontispiece and Vignette by J. A. CHRISTIE.
Sally Dows, &c. With 47 Illustrations by W. D. ALMOND and others.
A Protegee of Jack Hamlin's. With 26 Illustrations by W. SMALL and others.
The Bell-Ringer of Angel's, &c. With 39 Illustrations by DUDLEY HARDY and others.
Clarence: A Story of the American War. With Eight Illustrations by A. JULE GOODMAN.

Post 8vo, illustrated boards, 2s. each.
Gabriel Conroy. | **The Luck of Roaring Camp**, &c.
An Heiress of Red Dog, &c. | **Californian Stories.**

Post 8vo, illustrated boards, 2s. each; cloth, 2s. 6d. each.
Flip. | **Maruja.** | **A Phyllis of the Sierras.**

Fcap. 8vo, picture cover, 1s. each.
Snow-Bound at Eagle's. | **Jeff Briggs's Love Story.**

Haweis (Mrs. H. R.), Books by.
The Art of Beauty. With Coloured Frontispiece and 91 Illustrations. Square 8vo, cloth bds., 6s.
The Art of Decoration. With Coloured Frontispiece and 74 Illustrations. Sq. 8vo, cloth bds., 6s.
The Art of Dress. With 32 Illustrations. Post 8vo, 1s.; cloth, 1s. 6d.
Chaucer for Schools. Demy 8vo, cloth limp, 2s. 6d.
Chaucer for Children. With 38 Illustrations (8 Coloured). Crown 4to, cloth extra, 3s. 6d.

Haweis (Rev. H. R., M.A.), Books by.
American Humorists: WASHINGTON IRVING, OLIVER WENDELL HOLMES, JAMES RUSSELL LOWELL, ARTEMUS WARD, MARK TWAIN, and BRET HARTE. Third Edition. Crown 8vo, cloth extra, 6s.
Travel and Talk, 1885-93-95: One Hundred Thousand Miles of Travel through America—New Zealand—Australia—Tasmania—Ceylon—The Paradises of the Pacific. With Photogravure Frontispieces. Two Vols., crown 8vo, cloth, 21s.

Hawthorne (Julian), Novels by.
Crown 8vo, cloth extra, 3s. 6d. each; post 8vo, illustrated boards, 2s. each.
Garth. | **Ellice Quentin.** | **Beatrix Randolph.** With Four Illusts.
Sebastian Strome. | | **David Poindexter's Disappearance.**
Fortune's Fool. | **Dust.** Four Illusts. | **The Spectre of the Camera.**

Post 8vo, illustrated boards, 2s. each.
Miss Cadogna. | **Love—or a Name.**
Mrs. Gainsborough's Diamonds. Fcap. 8vo, illustrated cover, 1s.

Hawthorne (Nathaniel).—Our Old Home. Annotated with Passages from the Author's Note-books, and Illustrated with 31 Photogravures. Two Vols., cr. 8vo, 15s.

Heath (Francis George).—My Garden Wild, and What I Grew There. Crown 8vo, cloth extra, gilt edges, 6s.

Helps (Sir Arthur), Works by. Post 8vo, cloth limp, 2s. 6d. each.
Animals and their Masters. | **Social Pressure.**
Ivan de Biron: A Novel. Crown 8vo, cloth extra, 3s. 6d.; post 8vo, illustrated boards, 2s.

Henderson (Isaac). — Agatha Page: A Novel. Cr. 8vo, cl., 3s. 6d.

Henty (G. A.), Novels by.
Rujub the Juggler. With Eight Illustrations by STANLEY L. WOOD. Crown 8vo, cloth, 3s. 6d.; post 8vo, illustrated boards, 2s.
Dorothy's Double. Crown 8vo, cloth, 3s. 6d.

Herman (Henry).—A Leading Lady. Post 8vo, bds., 2s.; cl., 2s. 6d.

Herrick's (Robert) Hesperides, Noble Numbers, and Complete Collected Poems. With Memorial-Introduction and Notes by the Rev. A. B. GROSART, D.D., Steel Portrait, &c. Three Vols., crown 8vo, cloth boards, 18s.

Hertzka (Dr. Theodor).—Freeland: A Social Anticipation. Translated by ARTHUR RANSOM. Crown 8vo, cloth extra, 6s.

Hesse-Wartegg (Chevalier Ernst von).—Tunis: The Land and the People. With 22 Illustrations. Crown 8vo, cloth extra, 3s. 6d.

Hill (Headon).—Zambra the Detective. Post 8vo, bds., 2s.; cl., 2s. 6d.

Hill (John), Works by.
Treason-Felony. Post 8vo, boards, 2s. | The Common Ancestor. Cr. 8vo. cloth, 3s. 6d.

Hindley (Charles), Works by.
Tavern Anecdotes and Sayings: Including Reminiscences connected with Coffee Houses, Clubs, &c. With Illustrations. Crown 8vo, cloth extra, 3s. 6d.
The Life and Adventures of a Cheap Jack. Crown 8vo, cloth extra, 3s. 6d.

Hodges (Sydney).—When Leaves were Green. 3 vols.,15s. net.

Hoey (Mrs. Cashel).—The Lover's Creed. Post 8vo, boards, 2s.

Holiday, Where to go for a. By E. P. SHOLL, Sir H. MAXWELL, Bart., M.P., JOHN WATSON, JANE BARLOW, MARY LOVETT CAMERON, JUSTIN H. McCARTHY, PAUL LANGE, J. W. GRAHAM, J. H. SALTER, PHŒBE ALLEN, S. J. BECKETT, L. RIVERS VINE, and C. F. GORDON CUMMING. Crown 8vo, 1s.; cloth, 1s. 6d.

Hollingshead (John).—Niagara Spray. Crown 8vo, 1s.

Holmes (Gordon, M.D.)—The Science of Voice Production and Voice Preservation. Crown 8vo, 1s.; cloth, 1s. 6d.

Holmes (Oliver Wendell), Works by.
The Autocrat of the Breakfast-Table. Illustrated by J. GORDON THOMSON. Post 8vo, cloth limp, 2s. 6d.—Another Edition, post 8vo, cloth, 2s.
The Autocrat of the Breakfast-Table and The Professor at the Breakfast-Table. In One Vol. Post 8vo, half-bound, 2s.

Hood's (Thomas) Choice Works in Prose and Verse. With Life of the Author, Portrait, and 200 Illustrations. Crown 8vo, cloth extra, 7s. 6d.
Hood's Whims and Oddities. With 85 Illustrations. Post 8vo, half-bound, 2s.

Hood (Tom).—From Nowhere to the North Pole: A Noah's Arkæological Narrative. With 25 Illustrations by W. BRUNTON and E. C. BARNES. Cr. 8vo, cloth, 6s.

Hook's (Theodore) Choice Humorous Works; including his Ludicrous Adventures, Bons Mots, Puns, and Hoaxes. With Life of the Author, Portraits, Facsimiles, and Illustrations. Crown 8vo, cloth extra, 7s. 6d.

Hooper (Mrs. Geo.).—The House of Raby. Post 8vo, boards, 2s.

Hopkins (Tighe).—''Twixt Love and Duty.' Post 8vo, boards, 2s.

Horne (R. Hengist). — Orion: An Epic Poem. With Photograph Portrait by SUMMERS. Tenth Edition. Crown 8vo, cloth extra, 7s.

Hungerford (Mrs., Author of ' Molly Bawn '), Novels by.
Post 8vo, illustrated boards, 2s. each : cloth limp, 2s. 6d. each.
A Maiden All Forlorn. | In Durance Vile. | A Mental Struggle.
Marvel. | A Modern Circe.
Crown 8vo, cloth extra, 3s. 6d. each ; post 8vo, illustrated boards, 2s. each : cloth limp, 2s. 6d. each.
Lady Verner's Flight. | The Red-House Mystery.
The Three Graces. With 6 Illustrations. Crown 8vo, cloth extra, 3s. 6d.
The Professor's Experiment. Three Vols., crown 8vo, 15s. net.
A Point of Conscience. Three Vols., crown 8vo, 15s. net.

Hunt's (Leigh) Essays: A Tale for a Chimney Corner, &c. Edited by EDMUND OLLIER. Post 8vo, half-bound, 2s.

Hunt (Mrs. Alfred), Novels by.
Crown 8vo, cloth extra, 3s. 6d. each ; post 8vo, illustrated boards, 2s. each.
The Leaden Casket. | Self-Condemned. | That Other Person.
Thornicroft's Model. Post 8vo, boards, 2s. | Mrs. Juliet. Crown 8vo, cloth extra, 3s. 6d.

Hutchison (W. M.).—Hints on Colt-breaking. With 25 Illustrations. Crown 8vo, cloth extra, 3s. 6d.

Hydrophobia: An Account of M. PASTEUR'S System ; The Technique of his Method, and Statistics. By RENAUD SUZOR, M.B. Crown 8vo, cloth extra, 6s.

Hyne (C. J. Cutcliffe).— Honour of Thieves. Cr. 8vo, cloth, 3s. 6d.

Idler (The): An Illustrated Magazine. Edited by J. K. JEROME. 1s. Monthly. The First EIGHT VOLS. are now ready, cloth extra, 5s. each ; Cases for Binding, 1s. 6d. each.

mpressions (The) of Aureole. Cheaper Edition, with a New Preface. Post 8vo, blush-rose paper and cloth, 2s. 6d.

ndoor Paupers. By ONE OF THEM. Crown 8vo, 1s. ; cloth, 1s. 6d.

ngelow (Jean).—Fated to be Free. Post 8vo, illustrated bds., 2s.

nnkeeper's Handbook (The) and Licensed Victualler's Manual. By J. TREVOR-DAVIES. Crown 8vo, 1s. ; cloth, 1s. 6d.

rish Wit and Humour, Songs of. Collected and Edited by A. PERCEVAL GRAVES. Post 8vo, cloth limp, 2s. 6d.

rving (Sir Henry): A Record of over Twenty Years at the Lyceum. By PERCY FITZGERALD. With Portrait. Crown 8vo, 1s. ; cloth, 1s. 6d.

ames (C. T. C.). — A Romance of the Queen's Hounds. Post 8vo, picture cover, 1s. ; cloth limp, 1s. 6d.

ameson (William).—My Dead Self. Post 8vo, bds., 2s. ; cl., 2s. 6d.

app (Alex. H., LL.D.).—Dramatic Pictures, &c. Cr. 8vo, cloth, 5s.

ay (Harriett), Novels by. Post 8vo, illustrated boards, 2s. each.
The Dark Colleen. | The Queen of Connaught.

efferies (Richard), Works by. Post 8vo, cloth limp, 2s. 6d. each.
Nature near London. | The Life of the Fields. | The Open Air.
*** Also the HAND-MADE PAPER EDITION, crown 8vo, buckram, gilt top, 6s. each.

The Eulogy of Richard Jefferies. By Sir WALTER BESANT. With a Photograph Portrait. Crown 8vo, cloth extra, 6s.

ennings (Henry J.), Works by.
Curiosities of Criticism. Post 8vo, cloth limp, 2s. 6d.
Lord Tennyson: A Biographical Sketch. With Portrait. Post 8vo, 1s. ; cloth, 1s. 6d.

erome (Jerome K.), Books by.
Stageland. With 64 Illustrations by J. BERNARD PARTRIDGE. Fcap. 4to, picture cover, 1s.
John Ingerfield, &c. With 9 Illusts. by A. S. BOYD and JOHN GULICH. Fcap. 8vo, pic. cov. 1s. 6d.
The Prude's Progress: A Comedy by J. K. JEROME and EDEN PHILLPOTTS. Cr. 8vo, 1s. 6d.

errold (Douglas).—The Barber's Chair; and The Hedgehog Letters. Post 8vo, printed on laid paper and half-bound, 2s.

errold (Tom), Works by. Post 8vo, 1s. ea. ; cloth limp, 1s. 6d. each.
The Garden that Paid the Rent.
Household Horticulture : A Gossip about Flowers. Illustrated.

esse (Edward).—Scenes and Occupations of a Country Life. Post 8vo, cloth limp, 2s.

ones (William, F.S.A.), Works by. Cr. 8vo, cl. extra, 7s. 6d. each.
Finger-Ring Lore : Historical, Legendary, and Anecdotal. With nearly 300 Illustrations. Second Edition, Revised and Enlarged.
Credulities, Past and Present. Including the Sea and Seamen, Miners, Talismans, Word and Letter Divination, Exorcising and Blessing of Animals, Birds, Eggs, Luck, &c. With Frontispiece.
Crowns and Coronations: A History of Regalia. With 100 Illustrations.

onson's (Ben) Works. With Notes Critical and Explanatory, and a Biographical Memoir by WILLIAM GIFFORD. Edited by Colonel CUNNINGHAM. Three Vols. crown 8vo, cloth extra, 6s. each.

osephus, The Complete Works of. Translated by WHISTON. Containing 'The Antiquities of the Jews' and 'The Wars of the Jews.' With 52 Illustrations and Maps. Two Vols., demy 8vo, half-bound, 12s. 6d.

Kempt (Robert).—Pencil and Palette: Chapters on Art and Artists. Post 8vo, cloth limp, 2s. 6d.

Kershaw (Mark). — Colonial Facts and Fictions: Humorous Sketches. Post 8vo, illustrated boards, 2s. ; cloth, 2s. 6d.

Keyser (Arthur).—Cut by the Mess. Crown 8vo, 1s. ; cloth, 1s. 6d.

King (R. Ashe), Novels by. Cr. 8vo, cl., 3s. 6d. ea.; post 8vo, bds., 2s. ea.
A Drawn Game. | 'The Wearing of the Green.'

Post 8vo, illustrated boards, 2s. each.

Passion's Slave. | Bell Barry.

Knight (William, M.R.C.S., and Edward, L.R.C.P.). — The
Patient's Vade Mecum: How to Get Most Benefit from Medical Advice. Cr. 8vo, 1s.; cl., 1s. 6d.

Knights (The) of the Lion : A Romance of the Thirteenth Century
Edited, with an Introduction, by the MARQUESS OF LORNE, K.T. Crown 8vo, cloth extra, 6s.

Lamb's (Charles) Complete Works in Prose and Verse, including
'Poetry for Children' and 'Prince Dorus.' Edited, with Notes and Introduction, by R. H. SHEPHERD. With Two Portraits and Facsimile of the 'Essay on Roast Pig.' Crown 8vo, half-bd., 7s. 6d.
The Essays of Elia. Post 8vo, printed on laid paper and half-bound, 2s.
Little Essays: Sketches and Characters by CHARLES LAMB, selected from his Letters by PERCY FITZGERALD. Post 8vo, cloth limp, 2s. 6d.
The Dramatic Essays of Charles Lamb. With Introduction and Notes by BRANDER MATTHEWS, and Steel-plate Portrait. Fcap. 8vo, half-bound, 2s. 6d.

Landor (Walter Savage).—Citation and Examination of William
Shakspeare, &c., before Sir Thomas Lucy, touching Deer-stealing, 19th September, 1582. To which
is added, **A Conference of Master Edmund Spenser** with the Earl of Essex, touching the
State of Ireland, 1595. Fcap. 8vo, half-Roxburghe, 2s. 6d.

Lane (Edward William).—The Thousand and One Nights, com
monly called in England **The Arabian Nights' Entertainments.** Translated from the Arabic
with Notes. Illustrated with many hundred Engravings from Designs by HARVEY. Edited by EDWARD
STANLEY POOLE. With Preface by STANLEY LANE-POOLE. Three Vols., demy 8vo, cloth, 7s. 6d. each.

Larwood (Jacob), Works by.
The Story of the London Parks. With Illustrations. Crown 8vo, cloth extra, 3s. 6d.
Anecdotes of the Clergy. Post 8vo, laid paper, half-bound, 2s.

Post 8vo, cloth limp, 2s. 6d. each.

Forensic Anecdotes. | Theatrical Anecdotes.

Lehmann (R. C.), Works by. Post 8vo, 1s. each; cloth, 1s. 6d. each.
Harry Fludyer at Cambridge.
Conversational Hints for Young Shooters: A Guide to Polite Talk.

Leigh (Henry S.), Works by.
Carols of Cockayne. Printed on hand-made paper, bound in buckram, 5s.
Jeux d'Esprit. Edited by HENRY S. LEIGH. Post 8vo, cloth limp, 2s. 6d.

Leland (C. Godfrey). — A Manual of Mending and Repairing.
With Diagrams. Crown 8vo, cloth, 5s.

Lepelletier (Edmond). — Madame Sans-Gène. Translated from
the French by JOHN DE VILLIERS. Crown 8vo, cloth extra, 3s. 6d.

Leys (John).—The Lindsays : A Romance. Post 8vo, illust. bds., 2s.

Lindsay (Harry).—Rhoda Roberts : A Welsh Mining Story. Crown
8vo, cloth, 3s. 6d.

Linton (E. Lynn), Works by.
Crown 8vo, cloth extra, 3s. 6d. each; post 8vo, illustrated boards, 2s. each.
Patricia Kemball. | Ione. | Under which Lord ? With 12 Illustrations
The Atonement of Leam Dundas. | 'My Love!' | Sowing the Wind.
The World Well Lost. With 12 Illusts. | Paston Carew, Millionaire and Miser.
The One Too Many.

Post 8vo, illustrated boards, 2s. each.
The Rebel of the Family. | With a Silken Thread.

Post 8vo, cloth limp, 2s. 6d. each.
Witch Stories. | Ourselves: Essays on Women.
Freeshooting: Extracts from the Works of Mrs. LYNN LINTON.

Lucy (Henry W.).—Gideon Fleyce : A Novel. Crown 8vo, cloth
extra, 3s. 6d. ; post 8vo, illustrated boards, 2s.

Macalpine (Avery), Novels by.
Teresa Itasca. Crown 8vo, cloth extra, 1s.
Broken Wings. With Six Illustrations by W. J. HENNESSY. Crown 8vo, cloth extra, 6s.

MacColl (Hugh), Novels by.
Mr. Stranger's Sealed Packet. Post 8vo, illustrated boards, 2s.
Ednor Whitlock. Crown 8vo, cloth extra, 6s.

Macdonell (Agnes).—Quaker Cousins. Post 8vo, boards, 2s.

MacGregor (Robert).—Pastimes and Players : Notes on Popular
Games. Post 8vo, cloth limp, 2s. 6d.

Mackay (Charles, LL.D.). — Interludes and Undertones; or,
Music at Twilight. Crown 8vo, cloth extra, 6s.

McCarthy (Justin, M.P.), Works by.

A History of Our Own Times, from the Accession of Queen Victoria to the General Election o 1880. Four Vols., demy 8vo, cloth extra, 12s. each.—Also a POPULAR EDITION, in Four Vols., crown 8vo, cloth extra, 6s. each.—And the JUBILEE EDITION, with an Appendix of Events to the end of 1886, in Two Vols., large crown 8vo, cloth extra, 7s. 6d. each.

A Short History of Our Own Times. One Vol., crown 8vo, cloth extra, 6s.—Also a CHEAP POPULAR EDITION, post 8vo, cloth limp, 2s. 6d.

A History of the Four Georges. Four Vols., demy 8vo, cl. ex., 12s. each. [Vols. I. & II. *ready.*

Crown 8vo, cloth extra, 3s. 6d. each ; post 8vo, illustrated boards, 2s. each ; cloth limp, 2s. 6d. each.

The Waterdale Neighbours.	**Donna Quixote.** With 12 Illustrations.
My Enemy's Daughter.	**The Comet of a Season.**
A Fair Saxon.	**Maid of Athens.** With 12 Illustrations.
Linley Rochford.	**Camiola:** A Girl with a Fortune.
Dear Lady Disdain.	**The Dictator.**
Miss Misanthrope. With 12 Illustrations.	**Red Diamonds.**

The Riddle Ring. Three Vols., 15s. net.

'**The Right Honourable.**' By JUSTIN McCARTHY, M.P., and Mrs. CAMPBELL PRAED. Crown 8vo, cloth extra, 6s.

McCarthy (Justin Huntly), Works by.

The French Revolution. (Constituent Assembly, 1789-91). Four Vols., demy 8vo, cloth extra, 12s. each. Vols. I. & II. *ready ;* Vols. III. & IV. *in the press.*

An Outline of the History of Ireland. Crown 8vo, 1s. ; cloth, 1s. 6d.

Ireland Since the Union : Sketches of Irish History, 1798-1886. Crown 8vo, cloth, 6s.

Hafiz in London : Poems. Small 8vo, gold cloth, 3s. 6d.

Our Sensation Novel. Crown 8vo, picture cover, 1s. ; cloth limp, 1s. 6d.

Doom : An Atlantic Episode. Crown 8vo, picture cover, 1s.

Dolly : A Sketch. Crown 8vo, picture cover, 1s. ; cloth limp, 1s. 6d.

Lily Lass : A Romance. Crown 8vo, picture cover, 1s. ; cloth limp, 1s. 6d.

The Thousand and One Days. With Two Photogravures. Two Vols., crown 8vo, half-bd., 12s.

A London Legend. Crown 8vo, cloth, 3s. 6d.

MacDonald (George, LL.D.), Books by.

Works of Fancy and Imagination. Ten Vols., 16mo, cloth, gilt edges, in cloth case, 21s. ; or the Volumes may be had separately, in Grolier cloth, at 2s. 6d. each.

Vol. I. WITHIN AND WITHOUT.—THE HIDDEN LIFE.

,, II. THE DISCIPLE.—THE GOSPEL WOMEN.—BOOK OF SONNETS.—ORGAN SONGS.

,, III. VIOLIN SONGS.—SONGS OF THE DAYS AND NIGHTS.—A BOOK OF DREAMS.—ROADSIDE POEMS.—POEMS FOR CHILDREN.

,, IV. PARABLES.—BALLADS.—SCOTCH SONGS.

,, V. & VI. PHANTASTES : A Faerie Romance. | Vol. VII. THE PORTENT.

,, VIII. THE LIGHT PRINCESS.—THE GIANT'S HEART.—SHADOWS.

,, IX. CROSS PURPOSES.—THE GOLDEN KEY.—THE CARASOYN.—LITTLE DAYLIGHT.

,, X. THE CRUEL PAINTER.—THE WOW O' RIVVEN.—THE CASTLE.—THE BROKEN SWORDS —THE GRAY WOLF.—UNCLE CORNELIUS.

Poetical Works of George MacDonald. Collected and Arranged by the Author. Two Vols., crown 8vo, buckram, 12s.

A Threefold Cord. Edited by GEORGE MACDONALD. Post 8vo, cloth, 5s.

Phantastes : A Faerie Romance. With 25 Illustrations by J. BELL. Crown 8vo, cloth extra, 3s. 6d.

Heather and Snow : A Novel. Crown 8vo, cloth extra, 3s. 6d. ; post 8vo, illustrated boards, 2s.

Lilith : A Romance. SECOND EDITION. Crown 8vo, cloth extra, 6s.

Maclise Portrait Gallery (The) of Illustrious Literary Charac-

ters : **85 Portraits** by DANIEL MACLISE : with Memoirs—Biographical, Critical, Bibliographical and Anecdotal—illustrative of the Literature of the former half of the Present Century, by WILLIAM BATES, B.A. Crown 8vo, cloth extra, 7s. 6d.

Macquoid (Mrs.), Works by. Square 8vo, cloth extra, 6s. each.

In the Ardennes. With 50 Illustrations by THOMAS R. MACQUOID.

Pictures and Legends from Normandy and Brittany. 34 Illusts. by T. R. MACQUOID.

Through Normandy. With 92 Illustrations by T. R. MACQUOID, and a Map.

Through Brittany. With 35 Illustrations by T. R. MACQUOID, and a Map.

About Yorkshire. With 67 Illustrations by T. R. MACQUOID.

Post 8vo, illustrated boards, 2s. each.

The Evil Eye, and other Stories.	**Lost Rose,** and other Stories.

Magician's Own Book, The : Performances with Eggs, Hats, &c.

Edited by W. H. CREMER. With 200 Illustrations. Crown 8vo, cloth extra, 4s. 6d.

Magic Lantern, The, and its Management : Including full Practical

Directions. By T. C. HEPWORTH. With 10 Illustrations. Crown 8vo, 1s. ; cloth, 1s. 6d.

Magna Charta : An Exact Facsimile of the Original in the British

Museum, 3 feet by 2 feet, with Arms and Seals emblazoned in Gold and Colours. 5s.

Mallory (Sir Thomas). — Mort d'Arthur : The Stories of King

Arthur and of the Knights of the Round Table. (A Selection.) Edited by B. MONTGOMERIE RAN-KING. Post 8vo, cloth limp, 2s.

Mallock (W. H.), Works by.
The New Republic. Post 8vo, picture cover, 2s.; cloth limp, 2s. 6d.
The New Paul & Virginia: Positivism on an Island. Post 8vo, cloth, 2s. 6d.
A Romance of the Nineteenth Century. Crown 8vo. cloth 6s.; post 8vo, illust. boards, 2s.

Poems. Small 4to, parchment, 8s.
Is Life Worth Living? Crown 8vo, cloth extra, 6s.

Mark Twain, Books by. Crown 8vo, cloth extra, 7s. 6d. each.
The Choice Works of Mark Twain. Revised and Corrected throughout by the Author. Wit
  Life, Portrait, and numerous Illustrations.
Roughing It; and The Innocents at Home. With 200 Illustrations by F. A. FRASER.
Mark Twain's Library of Humour. With 197 Illustrations.

  Crown 8vo, cloth extra (illustrated), 7s. 6d. each; post 8vo, illustrated boards, 2s. each.
The Innocents Abroad; or, The New Pilgrim s Progress. With 234 Illustrations. (The Two Shi
  ling Edition is entitled **Mark Twain's Pleasure Trip.)**
The Gilded Age. By MARK TWAIN and C. D. WARNER. With 212 Illustrations.
The Adventures of Tom Sawyer. With 111 Illustrations.
A Tramp Abroad. With 314 Illustrations.
The Prince and the Pauper. With 190 Illustrations.
Life on the Mississippi. With 300 Illustrations.
The Adventures of Huckleberry Finn. With 174 Illustrations by E. W. KEMBLE.
A Yankee at the Court of King Arthur. With 220 Illustrations by DAN BEARD.

  Crown 8vo, cloth extra, 3s. 6d. each.
The American Claimant. With 81 Illustrations by HAL HURST and others.
Tom Sawyer Abroad. With 26 Illustrations by DAN. BEARD.
Pudd'nhead Wilson. With Portrait and Six IIIlustrations by LOUIS LOEB.
Tom Sawyer, Detective, &c. With numerous Illustrations.   [Shortly

The £1,000,000 Bank-Note. Crown 8vo, cloth, 3s. 6d.; post 8vo, picture boards 2s.

  Post 8vo, illustrated boards, 2s. each.
The Stolen White Elephant. | **Mark Twain's Sketches.**

Personal Recollections of Joan of Arc. By the SIEUR LOUIS DE CONTE. Edited by
  MARK TWAIN. With Twelve Illustrations by F. V. DU MOND. Crown 8vo, cloth, 6s.

Marks (H. S., R.A.), Pen and Pencil Sketches by. With Four
  Photogravures and 126 Illustrations. Two Vols. demy 8vo, cloth, 32s.

Marlowe's Works. Including his Translations. Edited, with Notes
  and Introductions, by Colonel CUNNINGHAM. Crown 8vo, cloth extra, 6s.

Marryat (Florence), Novels by. Post 8vo, illust. boards, 2s. each.
A Harvest of Wild Oats. | **Fighting the Air.**
Open! Sesame! | **Written in Fire.**

Massinger's Plays. From the Text of WILLIAM GIFFORD. Edited
  by Col. CUNNINGHAM. Crown 8vo, cloth extra, 6s.

Masterman (J.).—Half-a-Dozen Daughters. Post 8vo, boards, 2s.

Matthews (Brander).—A Secret of the Sea, &c. Post 8vo, illus-
  trated boards, 2s.; cloth limp, 2s. 6d.

Mayhew (Henry).—London Characters, and the Humorous Side
  of London Life. With numerous Illustrations. Crown 8vo, cloth, 3s. 6d.

Meade (L. T.), Novels by.
A Soldier of Fortune. Crown 8vo, cloth, 3s. 6d.; post 8vo, illustrated boards, 2s.
In an Iron Grip. Crown 8vo. cloth, 3s. 6d.
The Voice of the Charmer. Three Vols., 15s. net.

Merrick (Leonard), Stories by.
The Man who was Good. Post 8vo, picture boards, 2s.
This Stage of Fools. Crown 8vo, cloth, 3s. 6d.

Mexican Mustang (On a), through Texas to the Rio Grande. By
  A. E. SWEET and J. ARMOY KNOX. With 265 Illustrations. Crown 8vo, cloth extra, 7s. 6d.

Middlemass (Jean), Novels by. Post 8vo, illust. boards, 2s. each.
Touch and Go. | **Mr. Dorillion.**

Miller (Mrs. F. Fenwick).—Physiology for the Young; or, The
  House of Life. With numerous Illustrations. Post 8vo, cloth limp, 2s. 6d.

Milton (J. L.), Works by. Post 8vo, 1s. each; cloth, 1s. 6d. each.
The Hygiene of the Skin. With Directions for Diet, Soaps, Baths, Wines, &c.
The Bath in Diseases of the Skin.
The Laws of Life, and their Relation to Diseases of the Skin.

Minto (Wm.).—Was She Good or Bad? Cr. 8vo, 1s.; cloth, 1s. 6d.

Mitford (Bertram), Novels by. Crown 8vo, cloth extra, 3s. 6d. each.
The Gun-Runner: A Romance of Zululand. With a Frontispiece by STANLEY L. WOOD.
The Luck of Gerard Ridgeley. With a Frontispiece by STANLEY L. WOOD.
The King's Assegai. With Six full-page Illustrations by STANLEY L. WOOD.
Renshaw Fanning's Quest. With a Frontispiece by STANLEY L. WOOD.

Molesworth (Mrs.), Novels by.
Hathercourt Rectory. Post 8vo, illustrated boards, 2s.
That Girl in Black. Crown 8vo, cloth, 1s. 6d.

Moncrieff (W. D. Scott-).—The Abdication: An Historical Drama.
With Seven Etchings by JOHN PETTIE, W. Q. ORCHARDSON, J. MACWHIRTER, COLIN HUNTER,
R. MACBETH and TOM GRAHAM. Imperial 4to, buckram, 21s.

Moore (Thomas), Works by.
The Epicurean; and Alciphron. Post 8vo, half-bound, 2s.
Prose and Verse; including Suppressed Passages from the MEMOIRS OF LORD BYRON. Edited
by R. H. SHEPHERD. With Portrait. Crown 8vo, cloth extra, 7s. 6d.

Muddock (J. E.) Stories by.
Stories Weird and Wonderful. Post 8vo, illustrated boards, 2s.; cloth, 2s. 6d.
The Dead Man's Secret. With Frontispiece by F. BARNARD. Post 8vo, picture boards, 2s.
From the Bosom of the Deep. Post 8vo, illustrated boards, 2s.
Maid Marian and Robin Hood. With 12 Illusts. by STANLEY WOOD. Cr. 8vo, cloth extra, 3s. 6d.
Basile the Jester. With Frontispiece by STANLEY WOOD. Crown 8vo, cloth, 3s. 6d.

Murray (D. Christie), Novels by.
Crown 8vo, cloth extra, 3s. 6d. each; post 8vo, illustrated boards, 2s. each.

A Life's Atonement.	A Model Father.	First Person Singular.
Joseph's Coat. 12 Illusts.	Old Blazer's Hero.	Bob Martin's Little Girl.
Coals of Fire. 3 Illusts.	Cynic Fortune. Frontisp.	Time's Revenges.
Val Strange.	By the Gate of the Sea.	A Wasted Crime.
Hearts.	A Bit of Human Nature.	In Direst Peril.
The Way of the World.		

Mount Despair, &c. With Frontispiece by GRENVILLE MANTON. Crown 8vo, cloth, 3s. 6d.
The Making of a Novelist: An Experiment in Autobiography. With a Collotype Portrait and
Vignette. Crown 8vo, art linen, 6s.

Murray (D. Christie) and Henry Herman, Novels by.
Crown 8vo, cloth extra, 3s. 6d. each; post 8vo, illustrated boards, 2s. each.

One Traveller Returns.	The Bishops' Bible.
Paul Jones's Alias, &c. With Illustrations by A. FORESTIER and G. NICOLET.	

Murray (Henry), Novels by.
Post 8vo, illustrated boards, 2s. each; cloth, 2s. 6d. each.

A Game of Bluff.	A Song of Sixpence.

Newbolt (Henry).—Taken from the Enemy. Fcp. 8vo, cloth, 1s. 6d.

Nisbet (Hume), Books by.
'Ball Up.' Crown 8vo, cloth extra, 3s. 6d.; post 8vo, illustrated boards, 2s.
Dr. Bernard St. Vincent. Post 8vo, illustrated boards, 2s.

Lessons in Art. With 21 Illustrations. Crown 8vo, cloth extra, 2s. 6d.
Where Art Begins. With 27 Illustrations. Square 8vo, cloth extra, 7s. 6d.

Norris (W. E.), Novels by. Crown 8vo, cloth, 3s. 6d. each.

Saint Ann's.	Billy Bellew. Frontispiece by F. H. TOWNSEND.

O'Hanlon (Alice), Novels by. Post 8vo, illustrated boards, 2s. each.

The Unforeseen.	Chance? or Fate?

Ouida, Novels by. Cr. 8vo, cl., 3s. 6d. ea.; post 8vo, illust. bds., 2s. ea.

Held in Bondage.	Folle-Farine.	Moths. | Pipistrello.
Tricotrin.	A Dog of Flanders.	In Maremma. | Wanda.
Strathmore.	Pascarel. | Signa.	Bimbi. | Syrlin.
Chandos.	Two Wooden Shoes.	Frescoes. | Othmar.
Cecil Castlemaine's Gage	In a Winter City.	Princess Napraxine.
Under Two Flags.	Ariadne. | Friendship.	Guilderoy. | Ruffino.
Puck. | Idalia.	A Village Commune.	Two Offenders.

Square 8vo, cloth extra, 5s. each.
Bimbi. With Nine Illustrations by EDMUND H. GARRETT.
A Dog of Flanders, &c. With Six Illustrations by EDMUND H. GARRETT.

Santa Barbara, &c. Square 8vo, cloth, 6s.; crown 8vo, cloth, 3s. 6d.; post 8vo, illustrated boards, 2s.
Under Two Flags. POPULAR EDITION. Medium 8vo, 6d.; cloth, 1s.

Wisdom, Wit, and Pathos, selected from the Works of OUIDA by F. SYDNEY MORRIS. Post
8vo, cloth extra, 5s.—CHEAP EDITION, illustrated boards, 2s.

Ohnet (Georges), Novels by. Post 8vo, illustrated boards, 2s. each.
Doctor Rameau. | A Last Love.
A Weird Gift. Crown 8vo, cloth, 3s. 6d.; post 8vo, picture boards, 2s.

Oliphant (Mrs.), Novels by. Post 8vo, illustrated boards, 2s. each.
The Primrose Path. | Whiteladies.
The Greatest Heiress in England.

O'Reilly (Mrs.).—Phœbe's Fortunes. Post 8vo, illust. boards, 2s.

Page (H. A.), Works by.
Thoreau: His Life and Aims. With Portrait. Post 8vo, cloth limp, 2s. 6d.
Animal Anecdotes. Arranged on a New Principle. Crown 8vo, cloth extra, 5s.

Pandurang Hari; or, Memoirs of a Hindoo. With Preface by Sir
BARTLE FRERE. Crown 8vo, cloth, 3s. 6d.; post 8vo, illustrated boards, 2s.

Pascal's Provincial Letters. A New Translation, with Historical
Introduction and Notes by T. M'CRIE, D.D. Post 8vo, cloth limp, 2s.

Paul (Margaret A.).—Gentle and Simple. Crown 8vo, cloth, with
Frontispiece by HELEN PATERSON, 3s. 6d.; post 8vo, illustrated boards, 2s.

Payn (James), Novels by.
Crown 8vo, cloth extra, 3s. 6d. each; post 8vo, illustrated boards, 2s. each.

Lost Sir Massingberd.
Walter's Word.
Less Black than We're Painted.
By Proxy. | For Cash Only.
High Spirits.
Under One Roof.
A Confidential Agent. With 12 Illusts.
A Grape from a Thorn. With 12 Illusts.

Holiday Tasks.
The Canon's Ward. With Portrait.
The Talk of the Town. With 12 Illusts.
Glow-Worm Tales.
The Mystery of Mirbridge.
The Word and the Will.
The Burnt Million.
Sunny Stories. | A Trying Patient.

Post 8vo, illustrated boards, 2s. each.

Humorous Stories. | From Exile.
The Foster Brothers.
The Family Scapegrace.
Married Beneath Him.
Bentinck's Tutor.
A Perfect Treasure.
A County Family.
Like Father, Like Son.
A Woman's Vengeance.
Carlyon's Year. | Cecil's Tryst.
Murphy's Master.
At Her Mercy.
The Clyffards of Clyffe.

Found Dead.
Gwendoline's Harvest.
A Marine Residence.
Mirk Abbey.
Some Private Views.
Not Wooed, But Won.
Two Hundred Pounds Reward.
The Best of Husbands.
Halves.
Fallen Fortunes.
What He Cost Her.
Kit: A Memory.
A Prince of the Blood.

In Peril and Privation. With 17 Illustrations. Crown 8vo, cloth, 3s. 6d.
Notes from the 'News.' Crown 8vo, portrait cover, 1s.; cloth, 1s. 6d.

Payne (Will).—Jerry the Dreamer. Crown 8vo, cloth, 3s. 6d.

Pennell (H. Cholmondeley), Works by. Post 8vo, cloth, 2s. 6d. ea.
Puck on Pegasus. With Illustrations.
Pegasus Re-Saddled. With Ten full-page Illustrations by G. DU MAURIER.
The Muses of Mayfair: Vers de Société. Selected by H. C. PENNELL.

Phelps (E. Stuart), Works by. Post 8vo, 1s. ea.; cloth, 1s. 6d. ea.
Beyond the Gates. | An Old Maid's Paradise. | Burglars in Paradise.

Jack the Fisherman. Illustrated by C. W. REED. Crown 8vo, 1s.; cloth, 1s. 6d.

Phil May's Sketch=Book. Containing 50 full-page Drawings. Imp.
4to, art canvas, gilt top, 10s. 6d.

Phipson (Dr. T. L.).—Famous Violinists and Fine Violins.
Crown 8vo, cloth, 5s.

Pirkis (C. L.), Novels by.
Trooping with Crows. Fcap. 8vo, picture cover, 1s.
Lady Lovelace. Post 8vo, illustrated boards, 2s.

Planche (J. R.), Works by.
The Pursuivant of Arms. With Six Plates and 209 Illustrations. Crown 8vo, cloth, 7s. 6d.
Songs and Poems, 1819-1879. With Introduction by Mrs. MACKARNESS. Crown 8vo, cloth, 6s.

Plutarch's Lives of Illustrious Men. With Notes and a Life of
Plutarch by JOHN and WM. LANGHORNE, and Portraits. Two Vols., demy 8vo, half-bound 10s. 6d.

Poe's (Edgar Allan) Choice Works in Prose and Poetry. With Introduction by CHARLES BAUDELAIRE. Portrait and Facsimiles. Crown 8vo, cloth, 7s. 6d.
The Mystery of Marie Roget, &c. Post 8vo, illustrated boards, 2s.

Pope's Poetical Works. Post 8vo, cloth limp, 2s.

Porter (John).—Kingsclere: An Autobiography. Edited by BYRON WEBBER. With Twenty-two full-page Illustrations. Demy 8vo, cloth decorated, 18s.

Praed (Mrs. Campbell), Novels by. Post 8vo, illust. bds., 2s. each.
The Romance of a Station. | The Soul of Countess Adrian.

Crown 8vo, cloth, 3s. 6d. each ; post 8vo, boards, 2s. each.
Outlaw and Lawmaker. | Christina Chard. With Frontispiece by W. PAGET.
Mrs. Tregaskiss. Three Vols., crown 8vo, 15s. net.

Price (E. C.), Novels by.
Crown 8vo, cloth extra, 3s. 6d. each ; post 8vo, illustrated boards, 2s. each.
Valentina. | The Foreigners. | Mrs. Lancaster's Rival.
Gerald. Post 8vo, illustrated boards, 2s.

Princess Olga.—Radna: A Novel. Crown 8vo, cloth extra, 6s.

Proctor (Richard A., B.A.), Works by.
Flowers of the Sky With 55 Illustrations. Small crown 8vo, cloth extra, 3s. 6d.
Easy Star Lessons. With Star Maps for every Night in the Year. Crown 8vo, cloth, 6s.
Familiar Science Studies. Crown 8vo, cloth extra, 6s.
Saturn and its System. With 13 Steel Plates. Demy 8vo, cloth extra, 10s. 6d.
Mysteries of Time and Space. With numerous Illustrations. Crown 8vo, cloth extra, 6s.
The Universe of Suns, &c. With numerous Illustrations. Crown 8vo, cloth extra, 6s.
Wages and Wants of Science Workers. Crown 8vo, 1s. 6d.

Pryce (Richard).—Miss Maxwell's Affections. Crown 8vo, cloth, with Frontispiece by HAL LUDLOW, 3s. 6d.; post 8vo, illustrated boards, 2s.

Rambosson (J.).—Popular Astronomy. Translated by C. B. PITMAN. With Coloured Frontispiece and numerous Illustrations. Crown 8vo, cloth extra, 7s. 6d.

Randolph (Lieut.-Col. George, U.S.A.).—Aunt Abigail Dykes: A Novel. Crown 8vo, cloth extra, 7s. 6d.

Reade's (Charles) Novels.
Crown 8vo, cloth extra, mostly Illustrated, 3s. 6d. each ; post 8vo, illustrated boards, 2s. each.

Peg Woffington. | Christie Johnstone.
It is Never Too Late to Mend.
The Course of True Love Never Did Run Smooth.
The Autobiography of a Thief; Jack of all Trades; and James Lambert.
Love Me Little, Love Me Long.
The Double Marriage.
The Cloister and the Hearth.

Hard Cash. | Griffith Gaunt.
Foul Play. | Put Yourself in His Place.
A Terrible Temptation.
A Simpleton. | The Wandering Heir.
A Woman-Hater.
Singleheart and Doubleface.
Good Stories of Men and other Animals.
The Jilt, and other Stories.
A Perilous Secret. | Readiana.

A New Collected LIBRARY EDITION, complete in Seventeen Volumes, set in new long primer type, printed on laid paper, and elegantly bound in cloth, price 3s. 6d. each, is now in course of publication. The volumes will appear in the following order:—

1. Peg Woffington; and Christie Johnstone.
2. Hard Cash.
3. The Cloister and the Hearth. With a Preface by Sir WALTER BESANT.
4. 'It is Never too Late to Mend.'
5. The Course of True Love Never Did Run Smooth; and Singleheart and Doubleface.
6. The Autobiography of a Thief; Jack of all Trades; A Hero and a Martyr; and The Wandering Heir.

7. Love Me Little, Love me Long.
8. The Double Marriage.
9. Griffith Gaunt.
10. Foul Play.
11. Put Yourself in His Place.
12. A Terrible Temptation. [August.
13. A Simpleton. [Sept.
14. A Woman-Hater. [Oct.
15. The Jilt, and other Stories; and Good Stories of Men & other Animals.[Nov.
16. A Perilous Secret. [Dec.
17. Readiana; & Bible Characters.[Jan. '97

POPULAR EDITIONS, medium 8vo, 6d. each : cloth, 1s. each.
'It is Never Too Late to Mend.' | The Cloister and the Hearth.
Peg Woffington; and Christie Johnstone.
'It is Never Too Late to Mend' and The Cloister and the Hearth in One Volume, medium 8vo, cloth, 2s.
Christie Johnstone. With Frontispiece. Choicely printed in Elzevir style. Fcap. 8vo, half-Roxb. 2s. 6d.
Peg Woffington. Choicely printed in Elzevir style. Fcap. 8vo, half-Roxburghe, 2s. 6d.
The Cloister and the Hearth. In Four Vols., post 8vo, with an Introduction by Sir WALTER BESANT, and a Frontispiece to each Vol., 14s. the set ; and the ILLUSTRATED LIBRARY EDITION, with Illustrations on every page, Two Vols., crown 8vo, cloth gilt, 42s. net.
Bible Characters. Fcap. 8vo, leatherette, 1s.
Selections from the Works of Charles Reade. With an Introduction by Mrs. ALEX. IRELAND. Crown 8vo, buckram, with Portrait, 6s. ; CHEAP EDITION, post 8vo, cloth limp, 2s. 6d.

Riddell (Mrs. J. H.), Novels by.
Weird Stories. Crown 8vo, cloth extra, 3s. 6d.; post 8vo, illustrated boards, 2s.
Post 8vo, illustrated boards, 2s. each.
The Uninhabited House. | Fairy Water.
The Prince of Wales's Garden Party. | Her Mother's Darling.
The Mystery in Palace Gardens. | The Nun's Curse. | Idle Tales.

Rimmer (Alfred), Works by. Square 8vo, cloth gilt, 7s. 6d. each.
Our Old Country Towns. With 55 Illustrations by the Author.
Rambles Round Eton and Harrow. With 50 Illustrations by the Author.
About England with Dickens. With 58 Illustrations by C. A. VANDERHOOF and A. RIMMER.

Rives (Amelie).—Barbara Dering. Crown 8vo, cloth extra, 3s. 6d.
post 8vo, illustrated boards, 2s.

Robinson Crusoe. By DANIEL DEFOE. With 37 Illustrations by
GEORGE CRUIKSHANK. Post 8vo, half-cloth, 2s.; cloth extra, gilt edges, 2s. 6d.

Robinson (F. W.), Novels by.
Women are Strange. Post 8vo, illustrated boards, 2s.
The Hands of Justice. Crown 8vo, cloth extra, 3s. 6d.; post 8vo, illustrated boards, 2s.

The Woman in the Dark. Two Vols., 10s. net.

Robinson (Phil), Works by. Crown 8vo, cloth extra, 6s. each.
The Poets' Birds. | The Poets' Beasts.
The Poets and Nature: Reptiles, Fishes, and Insects.

Rochefoucauld's Maxims and Moral Reflections. With Notes
and an Introductory Essay by SAINTE-BEUVE. Post 8vo, cloth limp, 2s.

Roll of Battle Abbey, The: A List of the Principal Warriors who
came from Normandy with William the Conqueror, 1066. Printed in Gold and Colours, 5s.

Rosengarten (A.).—A Handbook of Architectural Styles. Translated by W. COLLETT-SANDARS. With 630 Illustrations. Crown 8vo, cloth extra, 7s. 6d.

Rowley (Hon. Hugh), Works by. Post 8vo, cloth, 2s. 6d. each.
Puniana: Riddles and Jokes. With numerous Illustrations.
More Puniana. Profusely Illustrated.

Runciman (James), Stories by. Post 8vo, bds., 2s. ea.; cl., 2s. 6d. ea.
Skippers and Shellbacks. | Grace Balmaign's Sweetheart.
Schools and Scholars.

Russell (Dora), Novels by. Crown 8vo, cloth, 3s. 6d. each.
A Country Sweetheart. | The Drift of Fate.

Russell (W. Clark), Books and Novels by.
Crown 8vo, cloth extra, 6s. each; post 8vo, illustrated boards, 2s. each; cloth limp, 2s. 6d. each.
Round the Galley-Fire. | A Book for the Hammock.
In the Middle Watch. | The Mystery of the 'Ocean Star.'
A Voyage to the Cape. | The Romance of Jenny Harlowe.

Crown 8vo, cloth extra, 3s. 6d. each; post 8vo, illustrated boards, 2s. each; cloth limp, 2s. 6d. each.
An Ocean Tragedy. | My Shipmate Louise. | Alone on a Wide Wide Sea.

Crown 8vo, cloth, 3s. 6d. each.
Is He the Man? | The Phantom Death, &c. With Frontispiece
The Good Ship 'Mohock.' | The Convict Ship.

On the Fo'k'sle Head. Post 8vo, illustrated boards, 2s.; cloth limp, 2s. 6d.
Heart of Oak. Three Vols., crown 8vo, 15s. net.
The Tale of the Ten. Three Vols., crown 8vo, 15s. net.

Saint Aubyn (Alan), Novels by.
Crown 8vo, cloth extra, 3s. 6d. each; post 8vo, illustrated boards, 2s. each.
A Fellow of Trinity. With a Note by OLIVER WENDELL HOLMES and a Frontispiece.
The Junior Dean. | The Master of St. Benedict's. | To His Own Master.
Orchard Damerel.

Fcap. 8vo, cloth boards, 1s. 6d. each.
The Old Maid's Sweetheart. | Modest Little Sara.

Crown 8vo, cloth extra, 3s. 6d. each.
In the Face of the World. | The Tremlett Diamonds.

Sala (George A.).—Gaslight and Daylight. Post 8vo, boards, 2s.

Sanson. — Seven Generations of Executioners: Memoirs of the
Sanson Family (1688 to 1847). Crown 8vo, cloth extra, 3s. 6d.

Saunders (John), Novels by.
Crown 8vo, cloth extra, 3s. 6d. each; post 8vo, illustrated boards, 2s. each.
Guy Waterman. | The Lion in the Path. | The Two Dreamers.

Bound to the Wheel. Crown 8vo, cloth extra, 3s. 6d.

Saunders (Katharine), Novels by.
Crown 8vo, cloth extra, 3s. 6d. each ; post 8vo, illustrated boards, 2s. each.

Margaret and Elizabeth. | Heart Salvage.
The High Mills. | Sebastian.

Joan Merryweather. Post 8vo, illustrated boards, 2s.
Gideon's Rock. Crown 8vo, cloth extra, 3s. 6d.

Scotland Yard, Past and Present: Experiences of Thirty-seven Years.
By Ex-Chief-Inspector CAVANAGH. Post 8vo, illustrated boards, 2s. ; cloth, 2s. 6d.

Secret Out, The : One Thousand Tricks with Cards ; with Entertaining Experiments in Drawing-room or 'White' Magic. By W. H. CREMER. With 300 Illustrations. Crown 8vo, cloth extra, 4s. 6d.

Seguin (L. G.), Works by.
The Country of the Passion Play (Oberammergau) and the Highlands of Bavaria. With Map and 37 Illustrations. Crown 8vo, cloth extra, 3s. 6d.
Walks in Algiers. With Two Maps and 16 Illustrations. Crown 8vo, cloth extra, 6s.

Senior (Wm.).—By Stream and Sea. Post 8vo, cloth, 2s. 6d.

Sergeant (Adeline).—Dr. Endicott's Experiment. Crown 8vo, buckram, 3s. 6d.

Shakespeare for Children : Lamb's Tales from Shakespeare.
With Illustrations, coloured and plain, by J. MOYR SMITH. Crown 4to, cloth gilt, 3s. 6d.

Sharp (William).—Children of To=morrow. Crown 8vo, cloth, 6s.

Shelley's (Percy Bysshe) Complete Works in Verse and Prose.
Edited, Prefaced, and Annotated by R. HERNE SHEPHERD. Five Vols., crown 8vo, cloth, 3s. 6d. each.
Poetical Works, in Three Vols. :
Vol. I. Introduction by the Editor : Posthumous Fragments of Margaret Nicholson ; Shelley's Correspondence with Stockdale ; The Wandering Jew ; Queen Mab, with the Notes ; Alastor, and other Poems ; Rosalind and Helen ; Prometheus Unbound ; Adonais, &c.
,, II. Laon and Cythna ; The Cenci ; Julian and Maddalo ; Swellfoot the Tyrant ; The Witch of Atlas ; Epipsychidion ; Hellas.
,, III. Posthumous Poems ; The Masque of Anarchy ; and other Pieces.
Prose Works, in Two Vols. :
Vol. I. The Two Romances of Zastrozzi and St. Irvyne : the Dublin and Marlow Pamphlets ; A Refutation of Deism ; Letters to Leigh Hunt, and some Minor Writings and Fragments.
,, II. The Essays ; Letters from Abroad ; Translations and Fragments, edited by Mrs. SHELLEY. With a Biography of Shelley, and an Index of the Prose Works.
*** Also a few copies of a LARGE-PAPER EDITION, 5 vols., cloth, £2 12s. 6d.

Sherard (R. H.).—Rogues: A Novel. Crown 8vo, 1s. ; cloth, 1s. 6d.

Sheridan (General P. H.), Personal Memoirs of. With Portraits, Maps, and Facsimiles. Two Vols., demy 8vo, cloth, 24s.

Sheridan's (Richard Brinsley) Complete Works, with Life and Anecdotes. Including his Dramatic Writings, his Works in Prose and Poetry, Translations, Speeches, and Jokes. With 10 Illustrations. Crown 8vo, half-bound, 7s. 6d.
The Rivals, The School for Scandal, and other Plays. Post 8vo, half-bound, 2s.
Sheridan's Comedies: The Rivals and The School for Scandal. Edited, with an Introduction and Notes to each Play, and a Biographical Sketch, by BRANDER MATTHEWS. With Illustrations. Demy 8vo, half-parchment, 12s. 6d.

Sidney's (Sir Philip) Complete Poetical Works, including all those in 'Arcadia.' With Portrait, Memorial-Introduction, Notes, &c., by the Rev. A. B. GROSART, D.D. Three Vols., crown 8vo, cloth boards, 18s.

Sims (George R.), Works by.
Post 8vo, illustrated boards, 2s. each ; cloth limp, 2s. 6d. each.

Rogues and Vagabonds. | Tales of To-day.
The Ring o' Bells. | Dramas of Life. With 60 Illustrations.
Mary Jane's Memoirs. | Memoirs of a Landlady.
Mary Jane Married. | My Two Wives.
Tinkletop's Crime. | Scenes from the Show.
Zeph : A Circus Story, &c. | The Ten Commandments: Stories.

Crown 8vo, picture cover, 1s. each ; cloth, 1s. 6d. each.
How the Poor Live ; and Horrible London.
The Dagonet Reciter and Reader : Being Readings and Recitations in Prose and Verse, selected from his own Works by GEORGE R. SIMS.
The Case of George Candlemas. | Dagonet Ditties. (From *The Referee*.)

Dagonet Abroad. Crown 8vo, cloth, 3s. 6d.

Signboards : Their History, including Anecdotes of Famous Taverns an-
Remarkable Characters. By JACOB LARWOOD and JOHN CAMDEN HOTTEN. With Coloured Front-
piece and 94 Illustrations. Crown 8vo, cloth extra, 7s. 6d.

Sister Dora : A Biography. By MARGARET LONSDALE. With Fou-
Illustrations. Demy 8vo, picture cover, 4d. ; cloth, 6d.

Sketchley (Arthur).—A Match in the Dark. Post 8vo, boards, 2s

Slang Dictionary (The) : Etymological, Historical, and Anecdotal
Crown 8vo, cloth extra, 6s. 6d.

Smart (Hawley).—Without Love or Licence : A Novel. Crow-
8vo, cloth extra, 3s. 6d. ; post 8vo, illustrated boards, 2s.

Smith (J. Moyr), Works by.
  The Prince of Argolis. With 130 Illustrations. Post 8vo, cloth extra, 3s. 6d.
  The Wooing of the Water Witch. With numerous Illustrations. Post 8vo, cloth, 6s.

Society in London. Crown 8vo, 1s. ; cloth, 1s. 6d.

Society in Paris: The Upper Ten Thousand. A Series of Letter
from Count PAUL VASILI to a Young French Diplomat. Crown 8vo, cloth, 6s.

Somerset (Lord Henry).—Songs of Adieu. Small 4to, Jap. vel., 6s

Spalding (T. A., LL.B.).— Elizabethan Demonology: An Essay
on the Belief in the Existence of Devils. Crown 8vo, cloth extra, 5s.

Speight (T. W.), Novels by.
Post 8vo, illustrated boards, 2s. each.

The Mysteries of Heron Dyke.	Back to Life.
By Devious Ways, &c.	The Loudwater Tragedy.
Hoodwinked ; & Sandycroft Mystery.	Burgo's Romance.
The Golden Hoop.	Quittance in Full.

Post 8vo, cloth limp, 1s. 6d. each.

A Barren Title.	Wife or No Wife?

Crown 8vo, cloth extra, 3s. 6d. each.

A Secret of the Sea.	The Grey Monk.

  The Sandycroft Mystery. Crown 8vo, picture cover, 1s.
  The Master of Trenance. Three Vols., crown 8vo, 15s. net.
  A Husband from the Sea. Post 8vo, illustrated boards, 2s.

Spenser for Children. By M. H. TOWRY. With Coloured Illustrations
by WALTER J. MORGAN. Crown 4to. cloth extra, 3s. 6d.

Stafford (John).—Doris and I, &c. Crown 8vo, cloth, 3s. 6d.

Starry Heavens (The) : A POETICAL BIRTHDAY BOOK. Royal 16mo,
cloth extra, 2s. 6d.

Stedman (E. C.), Works by. Crown 8vo, cloth extra, 9s. each.
  Victorian Poets. | The Poets of America.

Stephens (Riccardo, M.B.).—The Cruciform Mark : The Strange
Story of RICHARD TREGENNA, Bachelor of Medicine (Univ. Edinb.) Crown 8vo, cloth, 6s.

Sterndale (R. Arm'tage).—The Afghan Knife : A Novel. Crown
8vo, cloth extra, 3s. 6d. ; pos 8vo, illustrated boards, 2s.

Stevenson (R. Louis), Works by. Post 8vo, cloth limp, 2s. 6d. ea.
  Travels with a Donkey. With a Frontispiece by WALTER CRANE.
  An Inland Voyage. With a Frontispiece by WALTER CRANE.

Crown 8vo, buckram, gilt top, 6s. each.
  Familiar Studies of Men and Books.
  The Silverado Squatters. With Frontispiece by J. D. STRONG.
  The Merry Men. | Underwoods: Poems.
  Memories and Portraits.
  Virginibus Puerisque, and other Papers. | Ballads. | Prince Otto.
  Across the Plains, with other Memories and Essays.
  Weir of Hermiston. (R. L. STEVENSON'S LAST WORK.)

  New Arabian Nights. Crown 8vo, buckram, gilt top, 6s. ; post 8vo, illustrated boards, 2s.
  The Suicide Club; and The Rajah's Diamond. (From NEW ARABIAN NIGHTS.) With
    Eight Illustrations by W. J. HENNESSY. Crown 8vo, cloth, 5s.
  The Edinburgh Edition of the Works of Robert Louis Stevenson. Twenty-seven
    Vols., demy 8vo. This Edition (which is limited to 1,000 copies) is sold only in Sets, the price of
    which may be learned from the Booksellers. The First Volume was published Nov., 1894.

  Songs of Travel. Crown 8vo, buckram, 5s.   [Shortly.

Stoddard (C. Warren).—Summer Cruising in the South Seas.
Illustrated by WALLIS MACKAY. Crown 8vo, cloth extra, 3s. 6d.

Stories from Foreign Novelists. With Notices by HELEN and
ALICE ZIMMERN. Crown 8vo, cloth extra, 3s. 6d.; post 8vo, illustrated boards, 2s.

Strange Manuscript (A) Found in a Copper Cylinder. Crown
8vo, cloth extra, with 19 Illustrations by GILBERT GAUL, 5s.; post 8vo, illustrated boards, 2s.

Strange Secrets. Told by PERCY FITZGERALD, CONAN DOYLE, FLOR-
ENCE MARRYAT, &c. Post 8vo, illustrated boards, 2s.

Strutt (Joseph). — The Sports and Pastimes of the People of
England; including the Rural and Domestic Recreations, May Games, Mummeries, Shows, &c., from
the Earliest Period to the Present Time. Edited by WILLIAM HONE. With 140 Illustrations. Crown
8vo, cloth extra, 7s. 6d.

Swift's (Dean) Choice Works, in Prose and Verse. With Memoir,
Portrait, and Facsimiles of the Maps in 'Gulliver's Travels.' Crown 8vo, cloth, 7s. 6d.
Gulliver's Travels, and **A Tale of a Tub.** Post 8vo, half-bound, 2s.
Jonathan Swift: A Study. By J. CHURTON COLLINS. Crown 8vo, cloth extra, 8s.

Swinburne (Algernon C.), Works by.

Selections from the Poetical Works of A. C. Swinburne. Fcap. 8vo, 6s.	**A Study of Shakespeare.** Crown 8vo, 8s.
Atalanta in Calydon. Crown 8vo, 6s.	**Songs of the Springtides.** Crown 8vo, 6s.
Chastelard: A Tragedy. Crown 8vo, 7s.	**Studies in Song.** Crown 8vo, 7s.
Poems and Ballads. FIRST SERIES. Crown 8vo, or fcap. 8vo, 9s.	**Mary Stuart:** A Tragedy. Crown 8vo, 8s.
	Tristram of Lyonesse. Crown 8vo, 9s.
Poems and Ballads. SECOND SERIES. Crown 8vo, 9s.	**A Century of Roundels.** Small 4to, 8s.
	A Midsummer Holiday. Crown 8vo, 7s.
Poems & Ballads. THIRD SERIES. Cr. 8vo, 7s.	**Marino Faliero:** A Tragedy. Crown 8vo, 6s.
Songs before Sunrise. Crown 8vo, 10s. 6d.	**A Study of Victor Hugo.** Crown 8vo, 6s.
Bothwell: A Tragedy. Crown 8vo, 12s. 6d.	**Miscellanies.** Crown 8vo, 12s.
Songs of Two Nations. Crown 8vo, 6s.	**Locrine:** A Tragedy. Crown 8vo, 6s.
George Chapman. (See Vol. II. of G. CHAP-MAN'S Works.) Crown 8vo, 6s.	**A Study of Ben Jonson.** Crown 8vo, 7s.
	The Sisters: A Tragedy. Crown 8vo, 6s.
Essays and Studies. Crown 8vo, 12s.	**Astrophel,** &c. Crown 8vo, 7s.
Erechtheus: A Tragedy. Crown 8vo, 6s.	**Studies in Prose and Poetry.** Cr.8vo, 9s.
A Note on Charlotte Bronte. Cr. 8vo, 6s.	**The Tale of Balen.** Crown 8vo, 7s.

Syntax's (Dr.) Three Tours: In Search of the Picturesque, in Search
of Consolation, and in Search of a Wife. With ROWLANDSON'S Coloured Illustrations, and Life of the
Author by J. C. HOTTEN. Crown 8vo, cloth extra, 7s. 6d.

Taine's History of English Literature. Translated by HENRY VAN
LAUN. Four Vols., small demy 8vo, cloth boards, 30s.—POPULAR EDITION, Two Vols., large crown
8vo, cloth extra, 15s.

Taylor (Bayard). — Diversions of the Echo Club: Burlesques of
Modern Writers. Post 8vo, cloth limp, 2s.

Taylor (Dr. J. E., F.L.S.), Works by. Crown 8vo, cloth, 5s. each.
The Sagacity and Morality of Plants: A Sketch of the Life and Conduct of the Vegetable
Kingdom. With a Coloured Frontispiece and 100 Illustrations.
Our Common British Fossils, and Where to Find Them. With 331 Illustrations.
The Playtime Naturalist. With 366 Illustrations.

Taylor (Tom). — Historical Dramas. Containing 'Clancarty,'
'Jeanne Dare,' ''Twixt Axe and Crown,' 'The Fool's Revenge,' 'Arkwright's Wife,' 'Anne Boleyn,'
'Plot and Passion.' Crown 8vo, cloth extra, 7s. 6d.
*** The Plays may also be had separately, at 1s. each.

Tennyson (Lord): A Biographical Sketch. By H. J. JENNINGS. Post
8vo, portrait cover, 1s.; cloth, 1s. 6d.

Thackerayana: Notes and Anecdotes. With Coloured Frontispiece and
Hundreds of Sketches by WILLIAM MAKEPEACE THACKERAY. Crown 8vo, cloth extra, 7s. 6d.

Thames, A New Pictorial History of the. By A. S. KRAUSSE.
With 340 Illustrations. Post 8vo, 1s.; cloth, 1s. 6d.

Thiers (Adolphe). — History of the Consulate and Empire of
France under Napoleon. Translated by D. FORBES CAMPBELL and JOHN STEBBING. With 36 Steel
Plates. 12 Vols., demy 8vo, cloth extra, 12s. each.

Thomas (Bertha), Novels by. Cr. 8vo, cl., 3s. 6d. ea.; post 8vo, 2s. ea.
The Violin-Player. | **Proud Maisie.**
Cressida. Post 8vo, illustrated boards, 2s.

Thomson's Seasons, and The Castle of Indolence. With Introduction by ALLAN CUNNINGHAM, and 48 Illustrations. Post 8vo, half-bound, 2s.

Thornbury (Walter), Books by.
The Life and Correspondence of J. M. W. Turner. With Illustrations in Colours. Crown 8vo, cloth extra, 7s. 6d.
         Post 8vo, illustrated boards, 2s. each.
Old Stories Re-told. | Tales for the Marines.

Timbs (John), Works by. Crown 8vo, cloth extra, 7s. 6d. each.
The History of Clubs and Club Life in London: Anecdotes of its Famous Coffee-houses, Hostelries, and Taverns. With 42 Illustrations.
English Eccentrics and Eccentricities: Stories of Delusions, Impostures, Sporting Scenes, Eccentric Artists, Theatrical Folk, &c. With 48 Illustrations.

Transvaal (The). By JOHN DE VILLIERS. With Map. Crown 8vo, 1s.

Trollope (Anthony), Novels by.
     Crown 8vo, cloth extra, 3s. 6d. each; post 8vo, illustrated boards, 2s. each.
The Way We Live Now. | Mr. Scarborough's Family.
Frau Frohmann. | The Land-Leaguers.
         Post 8vo, illustrated boards, 2s. each.
Kept in the Dark. | The American Senator.
The Golden Lion of Granpere. | John Caldigate. | Marion Fay.

Trollope (Frances E.), Novels by.
     Crown 8vo, cloth extra, 3s. 6d. each; post 8vo, illustrated boards, 2s. each.
Like Ships Upon the Sea. | Mabel's Progress. | Anne Furness.

Trollope (T. A.).—Diamond Cut Diamond. Post 8vo, illust. bds., 2s.

Trowbridge (J. T.).—Farnell's Folly. Post 8vo, illust. boards, 2s.

Tytler (C. C. Fraser-).—Mistress Judith: A Novel. Crown 8vo, cloth extra, 3s. 6d.; post 8vo, illustrated boards, 2s.

Tytler (Sarah), Novels by.
     Crown 8vo, cloth extra, 3s. 6d. each; post 8vo, illustrated boards, 2s. each.
Lady Bell. | Buried Diamonds. | The Blackhall Ghosts.
         Post 8vo, illustrated boards, 2s. each.
What She Came Through. | The Huguenot Family.
Citoyenne Jacqueline. | Noblesse Oblige.
The Bride's Pass. | Beauty and the Beast.
Saint Mungo's City. | Disappeared.
The Macdonald Lass. With Frontispiece. Crown 8vo, cloth, 3s. 6d.

Upward (Allen), Novels by.
The Queen Against Owen. Crown 8vo, cloth, with Frontispiece, 3s. 6d.; post 8vo, boards, 2s.
The Prince of Balkistan. Crown 8vo, cloth extra, 3s. 6d.
A Crown of Straw. Crown 8vo, cloth, 6s.

Vashti and Esther. By the Writer of 'Belle's' Letters in *The World.* Crown 8vo, cloth extra, 3s. 6d.

Villari (Linda).—A Double Bond: A Story. Fcap. 8vo, 1s.

Vizetelly (Ernest A.).—The Scorpion: A Romance of Spain. With a Frontispiece. Crown 8vo, cloth extra, 3s. 6d.

Waller (S. E.).—Sebastiani's Secret. With Twelve full-page Illustrations by the Author. Crown 8vo, cloth, 6s.   [*Shortly.*

Walton and Cotton's Complete Angler; or, The Contemplative Man's Recreation, by IZAAK WALTON; and Instructions How to Angle, for a Trout or Grayling in a clear Stream, by CHARLES COTTON. With Memoirs and Notes by Sir HARRIS NICOLAS, and 61 Illustrations. Crown 8vo, cloth antique, 7s. 6d.

Walt Whitman, Poems by. Edited, with Introduction, by WILLIAM M. ROSSETTI. With Portrait. Crown 8vo, hand-made paper and buckram, 6s.

Ward (Herbert), Books by.
Five Years with the Congo Cannibals. With 92 Illustrations. Royal 8vo, cloth, 14s.
My Life with Stanley's Rear Guard. With Map. Post 8vo, 1s.; cloth, 1s. 6d.

Walford (Edward, M.A.), Works by.

Walford's County Families of the United Kingdom (1898). Containing the Descent, Birth, Marriage, Education, &c., of 12,000 Heads of Families, their Heirs, Offices, Addresses, Clubs, &c. Royal 8vo, cloth gilt, 50s.

Walford's Shilling Peerage (1898). Containing a List of the House of Lords, Scotch and Irish Peers, &c. 32mo, cloth, 1s.

Walford's Shilling Baronetage (1898). Containing a List of the Baronets of the United Kingdom, Biographical Notices, Addresses, &c. 32mo, cloth, 1s.

Walford's Shilling Knightage (1896). Containing a List of the Knights of the United Kingdom, Biographical Notices, Addresses, &c. 32mo, cloth, 1s.

Walford's Shilling House of Commons (1896). Containing a List of all the Members of the New Parliament, their Addresses, Clubs, &c. 32mo, cloth, 1s.

Walford's Complete Peerage, Baronetage, Knightage, and House of Commons (1898). Royal 32mo, cloth, gilt edges, 5s.

Tales of our Great Families. Crown 8vo, cloth extra, 3s. 6d.

Warner (Charles Dudley).—A Roundabout Journey. Crown 8vo, cloth extra, 6s.

Warrant to Execute Charles I. A Facsimile, with the 59 Signatures and Seals. Printed on paper 22 in. by 14 in. 2s.

Warrant to Execute Mary Queen of Scots. A Facsimile, including Queen Elizabeth's Signature and the Great Seal. 2s.

Washington's (George) Rules of Civility Traced to their Sources and Restored by MONCURE D. CONWAY. Fcap. 8vo, Japanese vellum, 2s. 6d.

Wassermann (Lillias), Novels by.
The Daffodils. Crown 8vo, 1s. ; cloth, 1s. 6d.

The Marquis of Carabas. By AARON WATSON and LILLIAS WASSERMANN. Post 8vo, illustrated boards, 2s.

Weather, How to Foretell the, with the Pocket Spectroscope. By F. W. CORY. With Ten Illustrations. Crown 8vo, 1s. ; cloth, 1s. 6d.

Webber (Byron).—Fun, Frolic, and Fancy. With 43 Illustrations by PHIL MAY and CHARLES MAY. Fcap. 4to, cloth, 5s.

Westall (William), Novels by.
Trust-Money. Post 8vo, illustrated boards, 2s. ; cloth, 2s. 6d.
Sons of Belial. Two Vols., crown 8vo, 10s. net.

Westbury (Atha).—The Shadow of Hilton Fernbrook: A Romance of Maoriland. Crown 8vo, cloth, 3s. 6d.

Whist, How to Play Solo. By ABRAHAM S. WILKS and CHARLES F. PARDON. Post 8vo, cloth limp, 2s.

White (Gilbert).—The Natural History of Selborne. Post 8vo, printed on laid paper and half-bound, 2s.

Williams (W. Mattieu, F.R.A.S.), Works by.
Science in Short Chapters. Crown 8vo, cloth extra, 7s. 6d.
A Simple Treatise on Heat. With Illustrations. Crown 8vo, cloth, 2s. 6d
The Chemistry of Cookery. Crown 8vo, cloth extra, 6s.
The Chemistry of Iron and Steel Making. Crown 8vo, cloth extra, 9s.
A Vindication of Phrenology. With Portrait and 43 Illusts. Demy 8vo, cloth extra, 12s. 6d.

Williamson (Mrs. F. H.).—A Child Widow. Post 8vo, bds., 2s.

Wills (C. J.).—An Easy-going Fellow. Crown 8vo, cloth, 6s.

Wilson (Dr. Andrew, F.R.S.E.), Works by.
Chapters on Evolution. With 259 Illustrations. Crown 8vo, cloth extra, 7s. 6d.
Leaves from a Naturalist's Note-Book. Post 8vo, cloth limp, 2s. 6d
Leisure-Time Studies. With Illustrations. Crown 8vo, cloth extra, 6s.
Studies in Life and Sense. With numerous Illustrations. Crown 8vo, cloth extra, 6s.
Common Accidents: How to Treat Them. With Illustrations. Crown 8vo, 1s. ; cloth, 1s. 6d.
Glimpses of Nature. With 35 Illustrations. Crown 8vo, cloth extra, 3s. 6d.

Winter (J. S.), Stories by. Post 8vo, illustrated boards, 2s. each ; cloth limp, 2s. 6d. each.
Cavalry Life. | **Regimental Legends.**

A Soldier's Children. With 34 Illustrations by E. G. THOMSON and E. STUART HARDY. Crown 8vo, cloth extra, 3s. 6d.

Wissmann (Hermann von). — My Second Journey through Equatorial Africa. With 92 Illustrations. Demy 8vo, cloth, 16s.

Wood (H. F.), Detective Stories by. Post 8vo, boards, 2s. each.
The Passenger from Scotland Yard. | The Englishman of the Rue Cain.

Wood (Lady).—Sabina: A Novel. Post 8vo, illustrated boards, 2s.

Woolley (Celia Parker).—Rachel Armstrong; or, Love and Theology. Post 8vo, illustrated boards, 2s.; cloth, 2s. 6d.

Wright (Thomas), Works by. Crown 8vo. cloth extra, 7s. 6d. each.
The Caricature History of the Georges. With 400 Caricatures, Squibs, &c.
History of Caricature and of the Grotesque in Art, Literature, Sculpture, and Painting. Illustrated by F. W. FAIRHOLT, F.S.A.

Wynman (Margaret).—My Flirtations. With 13 Illustrations by J. BERNARD PARTRIDGE. Post 8vo, cloth, 3s. 6d.

Yates (Edmund), Novels by. Post 8vo, illustrated boards, 2s. each.
Land at Last. | The Forlorn Hope. | Castaway.

Zangwill (I.). — Ghetto Tragedies. With Three Illustrations by A. S. BOYD. Fcap. 8vo, picture cover, 1s. net.

Zola (Emile), Novels by. Crown 8vo, cloth extra, 3s. 6d. each.
The Fat and the Thin. Translated by ERNEST A. VIZETELLY.
Money. Translated by ERNEST A. VIZETELLY.
The Downfall. Translated by E. A. VIZETELLY.
The Dream. Translated by ELIZA CHASE. With Eight Illustrations by JEANNIOT.
Doctor Pascal. Translated by E. A. VIZETELLY. With Portrait of the Author.
Lourdes. Translated by ERNEST A. VIZETELLY.
Rome. Translated by ERNEST A. VIZETELLY.

SOME BOOKS CLASSIFIED IN SERIES.

. *For fuller cataloguing, see alphabetical arrangement, pp. 1-26.*

The Mayfair Library. Post 8vo, cloth limp, 2s. 6d. per Volume.

A Journey Round My Room. By X. DE MAISTRE. Translated by Sir HENRY ATTWELL.
Quips and Quiddities. By W. D. ADAMS.
The Agony Column of 'The Times.'
Melancholy Anatomised: Abridgment of BURTON.
Poetical Ingenuities. By W. T. DOBSON.
The Cupboard Papers. By FIN-BEC.
W. S. Gilbert's Plays. Three Series.
Songs of Irish Wit and Humour.
Animals and their Masters. By Sir A. HELPS.
Social Pressure. By Sir A. HELPS.
Curiosities of Criticism. By H. J. JENNINGS.
The Autocrat of the Breakfast-Table. By OLIVER WENDELL HOLMES.
Pencil and Palette. By R. KEMPT.
Little Essays: from LAMB'S LETTERS.
Forensic Anecdotes. By JACOB LARWOOD.

Theatrical Anecdotes. By JACOB LARWOOD.
Jeux d'Esprit. Edited by HENRY S. LEIGH.
Witch Stories. By E. LYNN LINTON.
Ourselves. By E. LYNN LINTON.
Pastimes and Players. By R. MACGREGOR.
New Paul and Virginia. By W. H. MALLOCK.
The New Republic. By W. H. MALLOCK.
Puck on Pegasus. By H. C. PENNELL.
Pegasus Re-saddled. By H. C. PENNELL.
Muses of Mayfair. Edited by H. C. PENNELL.
Thoreau: His Life and Aims. By H. A. PAGE.
Puniana. By Hon. HUGH ROWLEY.
More Puniana. By Hon. HUGH ROWLEY.
The Philosophy of Handwriting.
By Stream and Sea. By WILLIAM SENIOR.
Leaves from a Naturalist's Note-Book. By Dr. ANDREW WILSON.

The Golden Library. Post 8vo, cloth limp, 2s. per Volume.

Diversions of the Echo Club. BAYARD TAYLOR.
Songs for Sailors. By W. C. BENNETT.
Lives of the Necromancers. By W. GODWIN.
The Poetical Works of Alexander Pope.
Scenes of Country Life. By EDWARD JESSE.
Tale for a Chimney Corner. By LEIGH HUNT.

The Autocrat of the Breakfast Table. By OLIVER WENDELL HOLMES.
La Mort d'Arthur: Selections from MALLORY.
Provincial Letters of Blaise Pascal.
Maxims and Reflections of Rochefoucauld.

The Wanderer's Library. Crown 8vo, cloth extra, 3s. 6d. each.

Wanderings in Patagonia. By JULIUS BEERBOHM. Illustrated.
Merrie England in the Olden Time. By G. DANIEL. Illustrated by ROBERT CRUIKSHANK.
Circus Life. By THOMAS FROST.
Lives of the Conjurers. By THOMAS FROST.
The Old Showmen and the Old London Fairs. By THOMAS FROST.
Low-Life Deeps. By JAMES GREENWOOD.
The Wilds of London. By JAMES GREENWOOD.

Tunis. By Chev. HESSE-WARTEGG. 22 Illusts.
Life and Adventures of a Cheap Jack.
World Behind the Scenes. By P. FITZGERALD.
Tavern Anecdotes and Sayings.
The Genial Showman. By E. P. HINGSTON.
Story of London Parks. By JACOB LARWOOD.
London Characters. By HENRY MAYHEW.
Seven Generations of Executioners.
Summer Cruising in the South Seas. By C. WARREN STODDARD. Illustrated.

THE PICCADILLY (3/6) NOVELS—*continued*.

By Mrs. CAMPBELL PRAED.
Outlaw and Lawmaker. | Christina Chard.

By E. C. PRICE.
Valentina. | Mrs. Lancaster's Rival.
The Foreigners. |

By RICHARD PRYCE.
Miss Maxwell's Affections.

By CHARLES READE.
It is Never Too Late to | Singleheart and Double-
  Mend. | face.'
The Double Marriage. | Good Stories of Men
Love Me Little, Love | and other Animals.
  Me Long. | Hard Cash.
The Cloister and the | Peg Woffington.
  Hearth. | Christie Johnstone.
The Course of True | Griffith Gaunt.
  Love. | Foul Play.
The Autobiography of | The Wandering Heir.
  a Thief. | A Woman-Hater.
Put Yourself in His | A Simpleton.
  Place. | A Perilous Secret.
A Terrible Temptation. | Readiana.
The Jilt. |

By Mrs. J. H. RIDDELL.
Weird Stories.

By AMELIE RIVES.
Barbara Dering.

By F. W. ROBINSON.
The Hands of Justice.

By DORA RUSSELL.
A Country Sweetheart. | The Drift of Fate.

By W. CLARK RUSSELL.
Ocean Tragedy. | Is He the Man ?
My Shipmate Louise. | The Good Ship 'Mo-
Alone on Wide Wide Sea | hock.'
The Phantom Death. | The Convict Ship.

By JOHN SAUNDERS.
Guy Waterman. | The Two Dreamers.
Bound to the Wheel. | The Lion in the Path.

By KATHARINE SAUNDERS.
Margaret and Elizabeth | Heart Salvage.
Gideon's Rock. | Sebastian.
The High Mills. |

By ADELINE SERGEANT.
Dr. Endicott's Experiment.

By HAWLEY SMART.
Without Love or Licence.

By T. W. SPEIGHT.
A Secret of the Sea. | The Grey Monk.

By ALAN ST. AUBYN.
A Fellow of Trinity. | In Face of the World.
The Junior Dean. | Orchard Damerel'.
Mast-r of St Benedict's. | The Tremlett Diamonds.
To his Own Master. |

By JOHN STAFFORD.
Doris and I.

By R. A. STERNDALE.
The Afghan Knife.

By BERTHA THOMAS.
Proud Maisie. | The Violin-Player.

By ANTHONY TROLLOPE.
The Way we Live Now. | Scarborough's Family.
Frau Frohmann. | The Land-Leaguers.

By FRANCES E. TROLLOPE.
Like Ships upon the | Anne Furness.
  Sea. | Mabel's Progress.

By IVAN TURGENIEFF, &c.
Stories from Foreign Novelists.

By MARK TWAIN.
The American Claimant. | Pudd'nhead Wilson.
The £1,000,000 Bank-note. | Tom Sawyer, Detective.
Tom Sawyer Abroad. |

By C. C. FRASER-TYTLER.
Mistress Judith.

By SARAH TYTLER.
Lady Bell. | The Blackhall Ghosts.
Buried Diamonds. | The Macdonald Lass.

By ALLEN UPWARD.
The Queen against Owen.
The Prince of Balkistan.

By E. A. VIZETELLY.
The Scorpion : A Romance of Spain.

By ATHA WESTBURY.
The Shadow of Hilton Fernbrook.

By JOHN STRANGE WINTER.
A Soldier's Children.

By MARGARET WYNMAN.
My Flirtations.

By E. ZOLA.
The Downfall. | Money. | Lourdes.
The Dream. | The Fat and the Thin.
Dr. Pascal. | Rome.

CHEAP EDITIONS OF POPULAR NOVELS.
Post 8vo, illustrated boards, 2s. each.

By ARTEMUS WARD.
Artemus Ward Complete.

By EDMOND ABOUT.
The Fellah.

By HAMILTON AÏDÉ.
Carr of Carrlyon. | Confidences.

By MARY ALBERT.
Brooke Finchley's Daughter.

By Mrs. ALEXANDER.
Maid, Wife or Widow ? | Valerie's Fate.

By GRANT ALLEN.
Philistia. | The Great Taboo.
Strange Stories. | Dumaresq's Daughter.
Babylon | Duchess of Powysland.
For Maimie's Sake. | Blood Royal.
In all Shades. | Ivan Greet's Master-
The Beckoning Hand. | piece.
The Devil's Die. | The Scallywag.
The Tents of Shem. | This Mortal Coil.

By E. LESTER ARNOLD.
Phra the Phœnician.

By SHELSLEY BEAUCHAMP.
Grantley Grange.

BY FRANK BARRETT.
Fettered for Life. | A Prodigal's Progress.
Little Lady Linton. | Found Guilty.
Between Life & Death. | A Recoiling Vengeance.
The Sin of Olga Zassou- | For Love and Honour.
  lich. | John Ford; and His
Folly Morrison. | Helpmate.
Lieut. Barnabas. | The Woman of the Iron
Honest Davie. | Bracelets.

By Sir W. BESANT and J. RICE.
Ready-Money Mortiboy | By Celia's Arbour.
My Little Girl. | Chaplain of the Fleet.
With Harp and Crown. | The Seamy Side.
This Son of Vulcan. | The Case of Mr. Lucraft.
The Golden Butterfly. | In Trafalgar's Bay.
The Monks of Thelema. | The Ten Years' Tenant.

By Sir WALTER BESANT.
All Sorts and Condi- | For Faith and Freedom.
  tions of Men. | To Call Her Mine.
The Captains' Room. | The Bell of St. Paul's.
All in a Garden Fair. | The Holy Rose.
Dorothy Forster. | Armorel of Lyonesse.
Uncle Jack. | S. Katherine's by Tower.
The World Went Very | Verbena Camellia Ste-
  Well Then. | phanotis.
Children of Gibeon. | The Ivory Gate.
Herr Paulus. | The Rebel Queen.

By AMBROSE BIERCE.
In the Midst of Life.

Two-Shilling Novels—*continued.*

By FREDERICK BOYLE.

Camp Notes. | Chronicles of No man's
Savage Life. | Land.

BY BRET HARTE.

Californian Stories. | Flip. | Maruja.
Gabriel Conroy. | A Phyllis of the Sierras.
The Luck of Roaring | A Waif of the Plains.
  Camp. | A Ward of the Golden
An Heiress of Red Dog. | Gate.

By HAROLD BRYDGES.

Uncle Sam at Home.

By ROBERT BUCHANAN.

Shadow of the Sword. | The Martyrdom of Ma-
A Child of Nature. | deline.
God and the Man. | The New Abelard.
Love Me for Ever. | Matt.
Foxglove Manor. | The Heir of Linne.
The Master of the Mine. | Woman and the Man.
Annan Water.

By HALL CAINE.

The Shadow of a Crime. | The Deemster.
A Son of Hagar.

By Commander CAMERON.

The Cruise of the 'Black Prince.'

By Mrs. LOVETT CAMERON.

Deceivers Ever. | Juliet's Guardian.

By HAYDEN CARRUTH.

The Adventures of Jones.

By AUSTIN CLARE.

For the Love of a Lass.

By Mrs. ARCHER CLIVE.

Paul Ferroll.
Why Paul Ferroll Killed his Wife.

By MACLAREN COBBAN.

The Cure of Souls. | The Red Sultan.

By C. ALLSTON COLLINS.

The Bar Sinister.

By MORT. & FRANCES COLLINS.

Sweet Anne Page. | Sweet and Twenty.
Transmigration. | The Village Comedy.
From Midnight to Mid- | You Play me False.
  night. | Blacksmith and Scholar
A Fight with Fortune. | Frances.

By WILKIE COLLINS.

Armadale. | AfterDark. | My Miscellanies.
No Name. | The Woman in White.
Antonina. | The Moonstone.
Basil. | Man and Wife.
Hide and Seek. | Poor Miss Finch.
The Dead Secret. | The Fallen Leaves.
Queen of Hearts. | Jezebel's Daughter.
Miss or Mrs.? | The Black Robe.
The New Magdalen. | Heart and Science.
The Frozen Deep. | 'I Say No!'
The Law and the Lady | The Evil Genius.
The Two Destinies. | Little Novels.
The Haunted Hotel. | Legacy of Cain.
A Rogue's Life. | Blind Love.

By M. J. COLQUHOUN.

Every Inch a Soldier.

By DUTTON COOK.

Leo. | Paul Foster's Daughter.

By C. EGBERT CRADDOCK.

The Prophet of the Great Smoky Mountains.

By MATT CRIM.

The Adventures of a Fair Rebel.

By B. M. CROKER.

Pretty Miss Neville. | Proper Pride.
Diana Barrington. | A Family Likeness.
'To Let.' | Village Tales and Jungle
A Bird of Passage. | Tragedies.

By W. CYPLES.

Hearts of Gold.

By ALPHONSE DAUDET.

The Evangelist; or, Port Salvation.

By ERASMUS DAWSON.

The Fountain of Youth.

By JAMES DE MILLE.

A Castle in Spain.

By J. LEITH DERWENT.

Our Lady of Tears. | Circe's Lovers.

By CHARLES DICKENS.

Sketches by Boz. | Nicholas Nickleby.
Oliver Twist.

By DICK DONOVAN.

The Man-Hunter. | In the Grip of the Law
Tracked and Taken. | From Information Re-
Caught at Last! | ceived.
Wanted! | Tracked to Doom.
Who Poisoned Hetty | Link by Link
  Duncan? | Suspicion Aroused.
Man from Manchester. | Dark Deeds.
A Detective's Triumphs | Riddles Read.

By Mrs. ANNIE EDWARDES.

A Point of Honour. | Archie Lovell.

By M. BETHAM-EDWARDS.

Felicia. | Kitty.

By EDWARD EGGLESTON.

Roxy.

By G. MANVILLE FENN.

The New Mistress. | The Tiger Lily.
Witness to the Deed.

By PERCY FITZGERALD.

Bella Donna. | Second Mrs. Tillotson.
Never Forgotten. | Seventy - five Brooke
Polly. | Street.
Fatal Zero. | The Lady of Brantome.

By P. FITZGERALD and others.

Strange Secrets.

By ALBANY DE FONBLANQUE.

Filthy Lucre.

By R. E. FRANCILLON.

Olympia. | King or Knave?
One by One. | Romances of the Law.
A Real Queen. | Ropes of Sand.
Queen Cophetua. | A Dog and his Shadow.

By HAROLD FREDERIC.

Seth's Brother's Wife. | The Lawton Girl.

Prefaced by Sir BARTLE FRERE.

Pandurang Hari.

By HAIN FRISWELL.

One of Two.

By EDWARD GARRETT.

The Capel Girls.

By GILBERT GAUL.

A Strange Manuscript.

By CHARLES GIBBON.

Robin Gray. | In Honour Bound.
Fancy Free. | Flower of the Forest.
For Lack of Gold. | The Braes of Yarrow.
What will World Say? | The Golden Shaft.
In Love and War. | Of High Degree.
For the King. | By Mead and Stream.
In Pastures Green. | Loving a Dream.
Queen of the Meadow. | A Hard Knot.
A Heart's Problem. | Heart's Delight.
The Dead Heart. | Blood-Money.

By WILLIAM GILBERT.

Dr. Austin's Guests. | The Wizard of the
James Duke. | Mountain.

By ERNEST GLANVILLE.

The Lost Heiress. | The Fossicker.
A Fair Colonist.

By Rev. S. BARING GOULD.

Red Spider. | Eve.

By HENRY GREVILLE.

A Noble Woman. | Nikanor.

By CECIL GRIFFITH.

Corinthia Marazion.

By SYDNEY GRUNDY.

The Days of his Vanity.

By JOHN HABBERTON.

Brueton's Bayou. | Country Luck.

By ANDREW HALLIDAY.

Every day Papers.

By Lady DUFFUS HARDY.

Paul Wynter's Sacrifice.

Two-Shilling Novels—*continued.*

By THOMAS HARDY.
Under the Greenwood Tree.

By J. BERWICK HARWOOD.
The Tenth Earl.

By JULIAN HAWTHORNE.

Garth.	Beatrix Randolph.
Ellice Quentin.	Love—or a Name.
Fortune's Fool.	David Poindexter's Dis-
Miss Cadogna.	appearance.
Sebastian Strome.	The Spectre of the
Dust.	Camera.

By Sir ARTHUR HELPS.
Ivan de Biron.

By G. A. HENTY.
Rujub the Juggler.

By HENRY HERMAN.
A Leading Lady.

By HEADON HILL.
Zambra the Detective.

By JOHN HILL.
Treason Felony.

By Mrs. CASHEL HOEY.
The Lover's Creed.

By Mrs. GEORGE HOOPER.
The House of Raby.

By TIGHE HOPKINS.
Twixt Love and Duty.

By Mrs. HUNGERFORD.

A Maiden all Forlorn.	A Modern Circe.
In Durance Vile.	Lady Verner's Flight.
Marvel.	The Red House Mystery
A Mental Struggle.	

By Mrs. ALFRED HUNT.

Thornicroft's Model.	Self-Condemned.
That Other Person.	The Leaden Casket.

By JEAN INGELOW.
Fated to be Free.

By WM. JAMESON.
My Dead Self.

By HARRIETT JAY.
The Dark Colleen. | Queen of Connaught.

By MARK KERSHAW.
Colonial Facts and Fictions.

By R. ASHE KING.

A Drawn Game.	Passion's Slave.
'The Wearing of the	Bell Barry.
Green.'	

By JOHN LEYS.
The Lindsays.

By E. LYNN LINTON.

Patricia Kemball.	The Atonement of Leam
The World Well Lost.	Dundas.
Under which Lord?	With a Silken Thread.
Paston Carew.	Rebel of the Family.
'My Love!'	Sowing the Wind.
Ione.	The One Too Many.

By HENRY W. LUCY.
Gideon Fleyce.

By JUSTIN McCARTHY.

Dear Lady Disdain.	Camiola.
Waterdale Neighbours.	Donna Quixote.
My Enemy's Daughter.	Maid of Athens.
A Fair Saxon.	The Comet of a Season.
Linley Rochford.	The Dictator.
Miss Misanthrope.	Red Diamonds.

By HUGH MACCOLL.
Mr. Stranger's Sealed Packet.

By GEORGE MACDONALD.
Heather and Snow.

By AGNES MACDONELL.
Quaker Cousins.

By KATHARINE S. MACQUOID.
The Evil Eye. | Lost Rose.

By W. H. MALLOCK.

A Romance of the Nine-	The New Republic.
teenth Century.	

By FLORENCE MARRYAT.

Open! Sesame!	A Harvest of Wild Oats.
Fighting the Air.	Written in Fire.

By J. MASTERMAN.
Half-a-dozen Daughters.

By BRANDER MATTHEWS.
A Secret of the Sea.

By L. T. MEADE.
A Soldier of Fortune.

By LEONARD MERRICK.
The Man who was Good.

By JEAN MIDDLEMASS.
Touch and Go. | Mr. Dorillion.

By Mrs. MOLESWORTH.
Hathercourt Rectory.

By J. E. MUDDOCK.

Stories Weird and Won-	From the Bosom of the
derful.	Deep.
The Dead Man's Secret.	

By D. CHRISTIE MURRAY.

A Model Father.	A Life's Atonement.
Joseph's Coat.	By the Gate of the Sea.
Coals of Fire.	A Bit of Human Nature.
Val Strange.	First Person Singular.
Old Blazer's Hero.	Bob Martin's Little Girl
Hearts.	Time's Revenges.
The Way of the World.	A Wasted Crime.
Cynic Fortune.	In Direst Peril.

By MURRAY and HERMAN.

One Traveller Returns.	The Bishops' Bible.
Paul Jones's Alias.	

By HENRY MURRAY.
A Game of Bluff. | A Song of Sixpence.

By HUME NISBET.
'Ball Up!' | Dr. Bernard St. Vincent.

By ALICE O'HANLON.
The Unforeseen. | Chance? or Fate?

By GEORGES OHNET.

Dr. Rameau.	A Weird Gift.
A Last Love.	

By Mrs. OLIPHANT.

Whiteladies.	The Greatest Heiress in
The Primrose Path.	England.

By Mrs. ROBERT O'REILLY.
Phœbe's Fortunes.

By OUIDA.

Held in Bondage.	Two Lit. Wooden Shoes.
Strathmore.	Moths.
Chandos.	Bimbi.
Idalia.	Pipistrello.
Under Two Flags.	A Village Commune.
Cecil Castlemaine's Gage	Wanda.
Tricotrin.	Othmar.
Puck.	Frescoes.
Folle Farine.	In Maremma.
A Dog of Flanders.	Guilderoy.
Pascarel.	Ruffino.
Signa.	Syrlin.
Princess Napraxine.	Santa Barbara.
In a Winter City.	Two Offenders.
Ariadne.	Ouida's Wisdom, Wit,
Friendship.	and Pathos.

By MARGARET AGNES PAUL.
Gentle and Simple.

By C. L. PIRKIS.
Lady Lovelace.

By EDGAR A. POE.
The Mystery of Marie Roget.

By Mrs. CAMPBELL PRAED
The Romance of a Station.
The Soul of Countess Adrian.
Outlaw and Lawmaker.
Christina Chard

By E. C. PRICE.

Valentina.	Mrs. Lancaster's Rival.
The Foreigners.	Gerald.

By RICHARD PRYCE.
Miss Maxwell's Affections.

Two-Shilling Novels—*continued.*

By JAMES PAYN.

Bentinck's Tutor.
Murphy's Master.
A County Family.
At Her Mercy.
Cecil's Tryst.
The Clyffards of Clyffe.
The Foster Brothers.
Found Dead.
The Best of Husbands.
Walter's Word.
Halves.
Fallen Fortunes.
Humorous Stories.
£200 Reward.
A Marine Residence.
Mirk Abbey.
By Proxy.
Under One Roof.
High Spirits.
Carlyon's Year.
From Exile.
For Cash Only.
Kit.
The Canon's Ward.

The Talk of the Town.
Holiday Tasks.
A Perfect Treasure.
What He Cost Her.
A Confidential Agent.
Glow-worm Tales.
The Burnt Million.
Sunny Stories.
Lost Sir Massingberd.
A Woman's Vengeance.
The Family Scapegrace.
Gwendoline's Harvest.
Like Father, Like Son.
Married Beneath Him.
Not Wooed, but Won.
Less Black than We're Painted.
Some Private Views.
A Grape from a Thorn.
The Mystery of Mirbridge.
The Word and the Will.
A Prince of the Blood.
A Trying Patient.

By CHARLES READE.

It is Never Too Late to Mend.
Christie Johnstone.
The Double Marriage.
Put Yourself in His Place
Love Me Little, Love Me Long.
The Cloister and the Hearth.
The Course of True Love.
The Jilt.
The Autobiography of a Thief.

A Terrible Temptation.
Foul Play.
The Wandering Heir.
Hard Cash.
Singleheart and Doubleface.
Good Stories of Men and other Animals.
Peg Woffington.
Griffith Gaunt.
A Perilous Secret.
A Simpleton.
Readiana.
A Woman-Hater.

By Mrs. J. H. RIDDELL.

Weird Stories.
Fairy Water.
Her Mother's Darling.
The Prince of Wales's Garden Party.

The Uninhabited House.
The Mystery in Palace. Gardens.
The Nun's Curse,
Idle Tales.

By AMELIE RIVES.

Barbara Dering.

By F. W. ROBINSON.

Women are Strange. | The Hands of Justice.

By JAMES RUNCIMAN.

Skippers and Shellbacks. | Schools and Scholars.
Grace Balmaign's Sweetheart.

By W. CLARK RUSSELL.

Round the Galley Fire.
On the Fo'k'sle Head.
In the Middle Watch.
A Voyage to the Cape.
A Book for the Hammock.
The Mystery of the 'Ocean Star.'

The Romance of Jenny Harlowe.
An Ocean Tragedy.
My Shipmate Louise.
Alone on a Wide Wide Sea.

By GEORGE AUGUSTUS SALA.

Gaslight and Daylight.

By JOHN SAUNDERS.

Guy Waterman. | The Lion in the Path.
The Two Dreamers.

By KATHARINE SAUNDERS.

Joan Merryweather.
The High Mills.
Heart Salvage.

Sebastian.
Margaret and Elizabeth.

By GEORGE R. SIMS.

Rogues and Vagabonds.
The Ring o' Bells.
Mary Jane's Memoirs.
Mary Jane Married.
Tales of To-day.
Dramas of Life.

Tinkletop's Crime.
Zeph.
My Two Wives.
Memoirs of a Landlady.
Scenes from the Show.
The 10 Commandments.

By ARTHUR SKETCHLEY.

A Match in the Dark.

By HAWLEY SMART.

Without Love or Licence.

By T. W. SPEIGHT.

The Mysteries of Heron Dyke.
The Golden Hoop.
Hoodwinked.
By Devious Ways.

Back to Life.
The Loudwater Tragedy.
Burgo's Romance.
Quittance in Full.
A Husband from the Sea.

By ALAN ST. AUBYN.

A Fellow of Trinity.
The Junior Dean.
Master of St. Benedict's

To His Own Master.
Orchard Damerel

By R. A. STERNDALE.

The Afghan Knife.

By R. LOUIS STEVENSON.

New Arabian Nights. | Prince Otto.

By BERTHA THOMAS.

Cressida.
Proud Maisie.

The Violin-Player.

By WALTER THORNBURY.

Tales for the Marines. | Old Stories Retold.

By T. ADOLPHUS TROLLOPE.

Diamond Cut Diamond.

By F. ELEANOR TROLLOPE.

Like Ships upon the Sea.

Anne Furness.
Mabel's Progress.

By ANTHONY TROLLOPE.

Frau Frohmann.
Marion Fay.
Kept in the Dark.
John Caldigate.
The Way We Live Now.

The Land-Leaguers.
The American Senator.
Mr. Scarborough's Family.
Golden Lion of Granpere

By J. T. TROWBRIDGE.

Farnell's Folly.

By IVAN TURGENIEFF, &c.

Stories from Foreign Novelists.

By MARK TWAIN.

A Pleasure Trip on the Continent.
The Gilded Age.
Huckleberry Finn.
Mark Twain's Sketches.
Tom Sawyer.
A Tramp Abroad.
Stolen White Elephant.

Life on the Mississippi.
The Prince and the Pauper.
A Yankee at the Court of King Arthur.
The £1,000,000 Bank-Note.

By C. C. FRASER-TYTLER.

Mistress Judith.

By SARAH TYTLER.

The Bride's Pass.
Buried Diamonds.
St. Mungo's City.
Lady Bell.
Noblesse Oblige.
Disappeared.

The Huguenot Family.
The Blackhall Ghosts.
What She Came Through
Beauty and the Beast.
Citoyenne Jaqueline.

By ALLEN UPWARD.

The Queen against Owen.

By AARON WATSON and LILLIAS WASSERMANN.

The Marquis of Carabas.

By WILLIAM WESTALL.

Trust-Money.

By Mrs. F. H. WILLIAMSON

A Child Widow.

By J. S. WINTER.

Cavalry Life. | Regimental Legends.

By H. F. WOOD.

The Passenger from Scotland Yard.
The Englishman of the Rue Cain.

By Lady WOOD.

Sabina.

By CELIA PARKER WOOLLEY.

Rachel Armstrong; or, Love and Theology

By EDMUND YATES.

The Forlorn Hope. | Castaway.
Land at Last.

OGDEN, SMALE AND CO. LIMITED, PRINTERS, GREAT SAFFRON HILL, E.C.

www.ingramcontent.com/pod-product-compliance
Lightning Source LLC
Chambersburg PA
CBHW030615270326
41927CB00007B/1190